With Women's Eyes

VISITORS TO THE NEW WORLD

1775–1918

Compiled and Edited by
MARION TINLING

UNIVERSITY OF OKLAHOMA PRESS
NORMAN

Library of Congress Cataloging-in-Publication Data

With women's eyes : visitors to the New World, 1775–1918 /
   compiled and edited by Marion Tinling.
      p.   cm.
      Originally published: Hamden, Conn. : Archon Books, 1993.
      Includes bibliographical references and index.
      ISBN 0–8061–3050–4 (pbk. : alk. paper)
      1. United States—Description and travel.   2. Women
   travelers—United States—History.   3. Travelers' writings.
   I. Tinling, Marion, 1904–
   [E161.5.W57   1999]
   917.304—dc21   98-37559
                                                                                    CIP

Oklahoma Paperbacks edition published 1999 by the University
of Oklahoma Press, Norman, Publishing Division of the University, by arrangement with Archon Books, an imprint of the Shoe
String Press, Inc., P.O. Box 657, 2 Linsley Street, North Haven,
Connecticut 06473-2517. Manufactured in the U.S.A. First printing of the University of Oklahoma Press edition, 1999.

1   2   3   4   5   6   7   8   9   10

Contents

Introduction

History Warm to the Touch

During the growing years of the American republic the country had a fascination for foreign visitors. They came from England, France, Sweden, and other European countries to see for themselves the strange New World. They wrote letters and kept journals recording their experiences in a democracy—an unprecedented and perhaps dangerous new political system. Americans read their books and reacted with approval or fury according to how much they agreed or disagreed with the writers.

Of course the visitors did not all see the same things or come to the same conclusions, as Frances Wright noted:

> It is somewhat curious to see how travellers contradict each other. One says things are white, and another that they are black; some write that the Americans have no religion, and others that they are a race of fanatics. One traveller tells us that they are so immersed in the affairs of the republic as not to have a word to throw at a stranger, and another, that they never think about politics at all and talk nonsense eternally (Frances Wright, *Views of Society and Manners in America*).

In 1775 America had been separated from mother Europe for long enough to develop noticeable differences in language and behavior. The country was teeming with energetic change, pride and self-regard. Frontiersmen pushed westward beyond the Alleghenies. During the first three-quarters of a century after independence, they reached the west coast and displaced the rule of the French, British, and Spanish. They built canals, bridges, roads, and railroads. They fashioned towns and cities and a national government, and developed a distinct culture. American society of the nineteenth century was anything but static. It is not surprising, therefore, that over the years travelers should see quite different aspects of the country and report quite different views.

Not a few of the Europeans who wrote about their experiences in the United States were women. Because they were women, they had unique opportunities to examine the domestic life of the Americans. They were able to get an inside view and a fresh perspective on society. Details of domestic life were as important to them as were public figures and events. They were interested in dress and hygiene, in living conditions, and in social institutions. They visited prisons, orphanages, asylums, and utopian communities. They described ordinary people, living ordinary lives; the ordinary living of extraordinary people; and ordinary people living extraordinary lives. All were American, though many were not conventionally thought of as American citizens.

An English traveler, Emily Pfeiffer, gently pointed out the value of seeing things through women's eyes:

> The lion has for so long been the painter, that he is apt too wholly to ignore the aspect which his favourite subject may take from the point of view of the lioness. If the latter will sometimes tell the truth, and tell, not what she thinks she ought to see, but what she really sees, many an intellectual picture which has hitherto satisfied the sense of mankind, may be found to be somewhat out of focus (Pfeiffer, *Flying Leaves from East and West*).

The bare facts of history have been well documented by men. They have carefully preserved and studied the letters and legal papers on which to base the story of the past. They treat of wars, political campaigns, agricultural and industrial developments. But historical facts gain a peculiar force when the details of family and workaday concerns are added. What appeared to men as secondary, trivial, and minor was of primary importance to women; women often noted a detail so important that men usually took it for granted. Thus we may find that the real history of America has largely been written by women. We may be surprised to discover that European women, coming from a different background and with different biases, have written some of the best of that history. They noticed details so familiar to American observers as to escape the historical record. When they penned their letters, kept their journals, or wrote their memoirs, they did not realize how much value future students would find in their observations. In writing for their contemporaries, they unwittingly created historical documents of genuine importance.

Each visitor who came to the United States had her own motives and expectations. Some were fleeing countries caught up in revolutionary changes of their own. Theresa Pulszky came with Louis Kossuth to elicit from sympathetic Americans support for the Hungarian Revolutionary cause. Madame Modjeska and her husband and friends left Poland under the hated Russians to seek Utopia in California. It did not turn out as they had imagined, but they discovered their Eden and enjoyed many years as enthusiastic Californians.

Others had purely personal reasons to leave their homes. The German Baroness von Riedesel was impelled by a belief that a woman's place was by the side of her husband, even if he was on the field of battle. Fanny Kemble sought a successful theater tour before returning to her London career. As it happened, she married and settled in the United States for a time and spent most of her later years as an American. The foolish Mrs. Trollope came from England to make money for her family. She failed as a businesswoman but her mean-spirited book about her two years in America launched a successful writing career back home.

Isabella Bird, a British clergyman's daughter, came to recover her health; all she needed was to get away from England and find herself. She said she wanted to "see things in their everyday dress." Harriet Martineau was also advised to go abroad to recover from the hard work of writing two treatises on political economy. But nothing could keep her from strenuous travel and many hours of recording her observations on every subject under the sun. Like Fredrika Bremer, the Swedish novelist, Martineau went armed with quill pens and bottles of ink.

A book of travel is the story of a quest. It is also a study of landscapes. Travel on the American continent drew forth lyric prose about its natural wonders—Niagara Falls, the Tennessee Valley, the Rockies, Yosemite, and the California redwoods. Writers enthused about fruited plains, purple mountains, and blossoming orchards. Not all, however, found nature reassuring. To some the forests were gloomy, the wetlands slimy and treacherous, the rocky heights dangerous. Ida Pfeiffer wondered that anyone should choose to go to the barren coast of California.

Marianne North came to find "tropical foliage"; she visited the New England coast and the noted people of Boston and Washington before escaping to California alone to paint giant redwoods. Trees and flowers delighted everyone; European women knew a surprising amount about botany, and were quick to see what was unique in the American natural world.

They were not so well versed on fauna as on flora, in part because European mythology populated the New World with fabulous creatures. The Scotswoman Janet Schaw expected to see lions, bears, tigers, and wolves in North Carolina; she had not anticipated alligators, which she equated with Revolutionaries. Theresa Longworth, from Ireland, did encounter a bear in the Yosemite mountains; it was compassionate enough not to attack her, instead frightening her into falling off a cliff.

One English humorist, Lady Theodora Guest, warns against certain creatures of the western prairies:

> There are, it seems, four venomous beasts on these prairies— first, the Tarantula, the enormous spider, ten inches across, on high legs, like a crab; and if he chooses to bite you, you die. Next, the Millepieds, nine inches or so long, like a centipede. If he runs over you, and you pretend to like it, all is well; but if you express the slightest objection to his freedom of action, he curls himself up, like a cantering caterpillar, sticks a few of his thousand feet into you, and—you die. The third is an obnoxious

monster, something like a lizard, called, as far as I can remember, a Kilomonster, who behaves in the same sort of way, with the same result; and, finally, the Rattlesnake. This latter reptile does not seem to weigh at all on the minds of the Aborigines, as they say if you let them alone they will not attack you, and they do not try to destroy them. A Rattlesnake coils up and throws himself at you, but as he always announces himself by three distinct rattles of his tail, and then can only fling himself his own length, and quite straight, it is supposed to be easy to avoid him. I am sure, though, if I had successfully avoided one, I should go straight home. His bite is not death, if you can get enough raw whisky and swallow it neat, right away (Guest, *A Round Trip in North America*).

Almost as much to be dreaded, for some travelers, were the Native Americans. The Baroness von Riedesel was told in England that she could be eaten by savages. However, she so overcame her fear that she was able to accept Indians in war paint as allies against the dreaded American soldiers her husband was fighting. She was surprised when the American officers turned out to be kind and noble gentlemen.

Most Europeans viewed Indians as curiosities of nature. The French Countess de La Tour du Pin became accustomed to seeing red-skinned couples promenading the roads near Albany in the buff. Anna Jameson became acquainted with Great Lakes Indians and was adopted by the Chippewas after an act of daring. Ida Pfeiffer, an amateur anthropologist who traveled the world seeking out wild tribes, was pleased to find some on the California coast with whom she could fraternize.

All travelers, naturally, spoke a good deal about how they got from one place to another. The preferred mode of getting about early in the century was by water, and many were the criticisms of crowded, dirty, noisy river boats, where the food and water were bad and the American habit of spitting right and left annoyed visitors. Land travel was even more difficult. America was slow to make roads, and the mud, dust, and roughness of trails over which one traveled by stage or carriage elicited heartfelt complaints.

Fortunately, most of the first travelers, especially the Englishwomen, knew horses and how to ride them. Isabella Bird survived an extraordinary ride alone through the Rocky Mountains, chiefly because she was a superb horsewoman. On the other hand, Rose Pender's remarks about the horses she saw at a western roundup deserves a guffaw. She considered the horses pitiful broken-spirited ponies and the cowboys rather poor riders.

Those who came after the railroads were built appreciated their comparative comfort and speed, although if one was going very far there were frequent transfers from one line to another. Lady Theodora Guest, in 1894, went by rail from East to West over nine railway lines in the same private car. Isabella Bird enjoyed her trip westward by rail, and was especially interested in the variety of travelers. She remarked on a democracy that might make traveling companions of the president of the Republic and the gentleman who shined your shoes in the morning.

Aside from difficulties of transportation, travelers found numerous problems as soon as they left the cities. Inns were usually described as filthy, crowded, and inhospitable. Food could not always be found, and sometimes it was the wrong kind. Many travelers did not like the manners of Americans, and they resented being asked, over and over, "How do you like our country?"

Few of the women traveled alone. Some came with husbands, many with maids. The Baroness von Riedesel's entourage included three babies, two maids, a groom and another manservant. Isabella Bird arrived in America with another woman, who soon went off by herself, abandoning the frail Isabella. But Bird liked independence and got along fine by herself. On a later trip, however, her go-it-alone policy landed her in as primitive a camp as one could imagine, in a cultural backwater even bleaker than the accommodations. Common sense and a capacity to ingratiate herself saw her through all difficulties.

Many women came especially to see how America treated women. They found the Declaration that "all men are created equal" and the Constitution that guaranteed the rights of all did not include slaves or women, never mind natives. They investigated careers and training available to women, residences for New York working girls, women's rights conventions, the bloomer fad, and the problems faced by rural wives.

Women's clubs—a phenomenon unique to America—elicited both favorable and unfavorable comment. Beatrice Webb, the noted English socialist who visited in 1898, spoke at a convention of the General Federation of Women's Clubs, formed in 1889. "It is difficult to estimate the worth of this 'Club Movement,' " Webb wrote:

> For the most part these clubs are simply mutual improvement societies; excuses for meetings at each others' houses, with something to talk about beyond servants and clothes. . . . We have no analogous movement in England. . . . To the women in the little towns and villages scattered over the vast plains of America, the Club Movement means the yearning for a wider life and brings to them a feeling of fellowship with other women, which may be the beginning of a desire for active citizenship (Webb, *American Diary*).

In 1917, Annie Smith also saw value in clubs for rural women, inasmuch as they served to bring women together for study and socializing.

Some of the visitors were simply interested in satisfying their curiosity and collecting material for travel books. They investigated slavery (before the Civil War), the Shakers, communal groups, and San Francisco's Chinatown. They were curious about the Utah Mormons, with their unfamiliar ideas about plural marriage.

Views of slavery ranged from the Hon. Amelia Murray's belief that all African Americans were merry and childlike to Fanny Kemble's chilling description of life on a Georgia plantation. In 1800 Americans had up to a million Negro slaves—a fifth of the total population. The entire economy of the South rested on the use of slave labor. Southerners as well as Northerners were aware of the dangers in the situation. They did not enjoy having foreigners add their criticisms.

No doubt the most meaningful aspect of foreign comment for today's reader is the reaction of Europeans to American democracy. A system of government of the people, by the people, and for the people was something new to Europeans, all of whom lived under authoritarian rule, and many of whom were struggling to attain freedom. Democracy had existed in ancient Athens and for brief periods at other times and in other places, but when America created its new institutions and backed them up with a written Constitution, the system was considered a bold experiment. It was, some thought, an experiment doomed to failure. In these days, with democracy the system of choice for emerging nations, it is fitting that attention should be given to what made that system unique, what made it work, and what is needed to preserve it.

Fanny Wright, a thoughtful British writer, pointed out in 1818 that "neither war nor legislation is the occupation of a body of men, but of the whole community: it occupies every head and every heart, rouses the whole energy, and absorbs the whole genius of the nation." She considered that the War of 1812 had united the country, "established the national independence and cemented the union." A much later visitor from France, the Countess de Bryas, was told in 1918 that the war was "making out of the inhabitants of the United States the American Nation: through it, unity is being created." The visitors' sense of the American nation, and of its self-creation, is much broader than that available to one who focuses only on public concerns of public men. Above all, what these visitors help us see is the way a broad spectrum of the American people actually lived their lives. In this we see both unity and diversity, but, most of all, vitality and energy.

The visit of the de Bryas sisters in 1918 is a fitting place to close. The war aroused the national spirit and created national unity. The United States became a world power. Foreign perceptions of the country changed. Its people were no longer regarded as Europeans transplanted to a New World, but as Americans. Still diverse, the country had acquired a distinctive and recognizable American culture.

Selections from the writings of twenty-six European women visitors are presented here. They were chosen as much for pleasurable reading as for specific content. Still they have much of substance to say. All but two of the women were writing in the nineteenth century, when educational opportunities for women were nothing like those available to their brothers. They are well-informed, however—often very well-informed—despite a few misconceptions about what they would find in America. They are also invariably literate, and express themselves forcefully, often wittily, and usually with imagination.

The texts are reprinted from the earliest editions available, without change, except that long passages are broken into paragraphs for easier reading. Ellipses indicate the omission of short sections; spaces mark longer breaks and changes of subject. Brackets enclose editorial insertions.

I owe a great deal to the late James Thorpe III, publisher of the 1993 edition of *With Women's Eyes*. He spent much time editing the manuscript with perception and a sense of humor that made our correspondence pleasurable and the book much better than it might have been. His untimely death in October 1994 was a loss to publishing. His widow, Diantha, saw the book through to publication and still carries on the work of the Shoe String Press.

1

Janet Schaw, Caught in a Revolution

Janet Schaw and her brother Alexander came to the United States from Edinburgh in 1775 to visit an older brother, Robert Schaw, who had long been settled on a North Carolina plantation. They were escorting three children of John Rutherfurd, another plantation owner related to the Schaw family. The children had been sent home to Scotland to be educated after the death of their mother.

CAPE FEAR RIVER, NORTH CAROLINA
FEBRUARY 14, 1775

At last America is in my view; a dreary Waste of white barren sand, and melancholy, nodding pines. In the course of many miles, no cheerful cottage has blest my eyes. All seems dreary, savage and desert; and was it for this that such sums of money, such streams of British blood have been lavished away? Oh, thou dear land, how dearly hast thou purchased this habitation for bears and wolves. Dearly has it been purchased, and at a prize far dearer still will it be kept. My heart dies within me, while I view it, and I am glad of an interruption by the arrival of a pilot-boat, the master of which appears a worthy inhabitant of the woods before us.

"Pray, Sir," said I to him, "does any body live hereabouts?"

"Hereabouts," returned he in a surly tone, "don't you see how thick it is settled."

He then pointed with his finger to a vast distance, and after some time, I really did observe a spot that seemed to be cut amongst the woods, and fancied that I saw something that resembled smoke. On this acknowledgment, he answered with a sort of triumph, "Ay, ay, I told you so, that there is Snow's plantation, and look ye there; don't ye see another? Why sure you are blind, it is not above five miles off."

I confessed I was short-sighted at least, for I really did not see it, and as he was now attending the casting the lead and reckoning our soundings, I troubled him with no more questions, but retired to the Cabin, not much elated with what I had seen.

SCHAWFIELD, MARCH 22, 1775

We have been these three or four days here, but this is the first time it has been in my power to write, but I have now sat down to bring up my Journal from leaving Brunswick; which we did last Friday, under the care of a Mr. Eagle, a young Gentleman just returned from England and who owns a very considerable estate in this province. The two brothers [Robert and Alexander] were to follow and be up with us in a few miles, which however they did not. We were in a Phaeton and four belonging to my brother, and as the roads are entirely level, drove on at good speed, our guide keeping by us and several Negro servants attending on horse back.

During the first few miles, I was charmed with the woods. The wild fruit trees are in full blossom; the ground under them covered with verdure and intermixed with flowers of various kinds made a pleasing Scene. But by and by it begins to grow dark, and as the idea of being benighted in the wilds of America was not a pleasing circumstance to an European female, I begged the servant to drive faster, but was told it would make little difference, as we must be many hours dark, before we could get clear of the woods, nor were our fears decreased by the stories Mr. Eagle told us of the wolves and bears that inhabited that part of the country.

Terrified at last almost to Agony, we begged to be carried to some house to wait for day-light, but we had drove at least two miles in that situation before Mr. Eagle recollected that a poor man had a very poor plantation at no great distance, if we could put up with it and venture to go off the road amongst the trees. This was not an agreeable proposition; however it was agreed to, and we soon found ourselves lost in the most impenetrable darkness, from which we could neither see sky, nor distinguish a single object.

We had not gone far in this frightful state, when we found the carriage stopt by trees fallen across the road, and were forced to dismount and proceed thro' this dreary scene on foot. All I had ever heard of lions, bears, tigers and wolves now rushed on my memory, and I secretly wished I had been made a feast to the fishes rather than to these monsters of the woods. With these thoughts in my head, I happened to slip my foot, and down I went and made no doubt I was sinking into the centre of the earth. It was not quite so deep however, for with little trouble Mr. Eagle got me safe up, and in a few minutes we came to an opening that showed us the sky and stars, which was a happy sight in our circumstances.

The carriage soon came up, and we again got into it. I now observed that the road was inclosed on both sides, and on the first turning the carriage made, we found ourselves in front of a large house from the windows of which beamed many cheerful tapers, and no sooner were we come up to the gate than a number of black servants came out with lights.

Mr. Eagle dismounted, and was ready to assist us, and now welcomed us to his house and owned that the whole was a plan only to get us to it, as he feared we might have made some objections; he having no Lady to receive us.

I had a great mind to have been angry, but was too happy to find myself safe, and every thing comfortable. We found the Tea-table set forth, and for the first time since our arrival in America had a dish of Tea.*

*Patriotic women here and elsewhere had given up drinking tea to protest the import tax placed on tea by the British; the tax was a cause of the Revolution.

We passed the evening very agreeably, and by breakfast next morning, the two brothers joined us. Mr. Eagle was my brother Bob's ward, and is a most amiable young man. We stayed all the forenoon with him, saw his rice mills, his indigo works and timber mills. The vast command they have of water makes those works easily conducted. Before I leave the country, I will get myself instructed in the nature of them, as well as the method of making the tar and turpentine, but at present I know not enough of them to attempt a description. . . .

But tho' I may say of this place what I formerly did of the West India Islands, that nature holds out to them every thing that can contribute to conveniency, or tempt to luxury, yet the inhabitants resist both, and if they can raise as much corn and pork, as to subsist them in the most slovenly manner, they ask no more; and as a very small proportion of their time serves for that purpose, the rest is spent in sauntering thro' the woods with a gun or sitting under a rustick shade, drinking New England rum made into grog, the most shocking liquor you can imagine. By this manner of living, their blood is spoil'd and rendered thin beyond all proportion, so that it is constantly on the fret like bad small beer, and hence the constant slow fevers that wear down their constitutions, relax their nerves and infeeble the whole frame.

Their appearance is in every respect the reverse of that which gives the idea of strength and vigor, and for which the British peasantry are so remarkable. They are tall and lean, with short waists and long limbs, sallow complexions and languid eyes, when not inflamed by spirits. Their feet are flat, their joints loose and their walk uneven.

These I speak of are only the peasantry of this country, as hitherto I have seen nothing else, but I make no doubt when I come to see the better sort, they will be far from this description. For tho' there is a most disgusting equality, yet I hope to find an American Gentleman a very different creature from the American clown. Heaven forfend else. . . .

I am sorry to say, however, that I have met with few of the men who are natives of the country, who rise much above my former description, and as their natural ferocity is now inflamed by the fury of an ignorant zeal, they are of that sort of figure, that I cannot look at them without connecting the idea of tar and feather. Tho' they have fine women and such as might inspire any man with sentiments that do honour to humanity, yet they know no such nice distinctions, and in this at least are real patriots. As the population of the country is all the view they have in what they call love, and tho' they often honour their black wenches with their attention, I sincerely believe they are excited to that crime by no other desire or motive but that of adding to the number of their slaves.

All the Merchants of any note are British and Irish, and many of them very genteel people. They all disapprove of the present proceedings. Many of them intend quitting the country as fast as their affairs will permit them, but are yet uncertain what steps to take. . . .

I left Wilmingtown and returned to Schawfield by water, which is a most delightful method of travelling thro' this Noble country, which indeed owes more favours to its God and king than perhaps any other in the known world and is equally ungrateful to both, to the God who created and bestowed them and to the king whose indulgent kindness has done every thing to render them of the greatest utility to the owners. . . .

Mrs. [Robert] Schaw . . . is connected with the best people in the country, and, I hope, will have interest enough to prevent her husband being ruined for not joining in a cause he so much disapproves. . . .

Things are going on with a high hand. A boat of provisions going to the king's ship has been stopped, and Mr. Hogg and Mr. Campbell, the contractors, ordered to send no more. Good God! what are the people at home about, to suffer their friends to be thus abused. Two regiments just now would reduce this province, but think what you will, in a little time, four times four will not be sufficient.

Every man is ordered to appear under arms. This the town's folks have been forced to comply with, tho' determined to go no further in a cause they so much disapprove. Melancholy clouds every honest face, while ferocity and insolence blaze in those of their enemies. . . . I will leave this letter to be sent, tho'

I risk tar and feather was it to be seen. Perhaps it may be the last I will ever write you at least from this part of the world. . . .*

Mr. Rutherfurd and Miss Rutherfurd . . . had been gone two days, and I was at Schawfield ready to set out, when to my no small surprise Miss Rutherfurd returned, and came to me there. The reason of which was, that they had met an express from Mr. [Archibald] Neilson, informing them and us that the Governor's house had been attacked, himself obliged to get down to the man-of-war, and send off his wife, sister and children in a little vessel, with directions to land them in the first safe port.

Field days are now appointed, and every man without distinction ordered to appear under arms and be drilled. Those who will not comply, must fly out of the country, and leave their effects behind them to the mercy of these people, whose kindness is little to be trusted. . . . My brother has been offered every thing but has refused every offer, and I tremble for his fate, but any thing rather than join these people.

You at home know nothing of the power of this country, nor will you believe it till you find it with a witness. I yesterday crushed an Alligator with my foot that in six months hence would be able to devour me. Six months ago a very little force would have done here, and even yet a proper exertion would do much towards resettling peace in these Southern provinces, tho' I am far from believing that the case with those further North. . . .

WILMINGTOWN

I went into the town, the entry of which I found closed up by a detachment of the soldiers; but as the officer immediately made way for me, I took no further notice of it, but advanced to the middle of the street, where I found a number of the first people in town standing together, who (to use Milton's phrase)

---

*"Tar and feather" refers to the punishment meted out by rebel mobs to tax collectors and those suspected of allegiance to the Crown.

seemed much impassioned. As most of them were my acquaintances, I stopped to speak to them, but they with one voice begged me for heaven's sake to get off the street, making me observe they were prisoners, adding that every avenue of the town was shut up, and that in all human probability some scene would be enacted very unfit for me to witness. I could not take the friendly advice, for I became unable to move and absolutely petrified with horror.

Observing however an officer with whom I had just dined, I beckoned him to me. He came, but with no very agreeable look, and on my asking him what was the matter, he presented a paper he had folded in his hand. If you will persuade them to sign this they are at liberty, said he, but till then must remain under this guard, as they must suffer the penalties they have just incurred. "And we will suffer every thing," replied one of them, "before we abjure our king, our country and our principles." . . . Oh Britannia, what are you doing, while your true obedient sons are thus insulted by their unlawful brethren; are they also forgot by their natural parents? . . .

The prisoners stood firm to their resolution of not signing the Test, till past two in the morning, tho' every threatening was used to make them comply; at which time a Message from the committee compromised the affair, and they were suffered to retire on their parole to appear next morning before them. This was not a step of mercy or out of regard to the Gentlemen; but they understood that a number of their friends were arming in their defence, and tho' they had kept about 150 ragamuffins still in town, they were not sure even of them; for to the credit of that town be it spoke, there are not five men of property and credit in it that are infected by this unfortunate disease. . . .

This will be delivered to you by my brother [Alexander], who has just stole up from the Sound to bid me, farewell. He has not an hour to stay: he goes home with despatches from the Governor. I am lost in confusion, this is unexpected indeed—oh heavens! Farewell.

News came from Boston of the Battle of Bunker Hill, fought on July 17. The British won, but at the cost of over a thousand casualties, many of them officers; the Americans lost a hundred. In September or October Miss Schaw, her maid, and the Rutherfurd children took refuge on board a ship sailing to Lisbon. With them was Mr. Neilson.

Farewell unhappy land, for which my heart bleeds in pity. Little does it signify to you, who are the conquered or who the victorious; you are devoted to ruin, whoever succeeds. Many years will not make up [for] these few last months of depredation, and yet no enemy has landed on their coast. Themselves have ruined themselves.

Janet Schaw, whose name does not appear on the title page of her manuscript journal (now in the British Museum) was identified only after painstaking research by her editors. They were, however, unable to fill in many details about her, particularly her life after her return to Scotland. The travelers arrived safely in Portugal, where they spent some months. Robert Schaw reluctantly accepted appointment as a colonel in the Revolutionary Army. Alexander Schaw never returned to the United States. He married, as her second husband, Fanny Rutherfurd, the eldest of the three children who had traveled with him to North Carolina. Janet Schaw's Journal *includes, besides the story of the trip to America, her voyages to the West Indies, Antigua and St. Christopher, and the sojourn in Lisbon.*

Janet Schaw, Journal of a Lady of Quality: Being the Narrative of a Journey from Scotland to the West Indies, North Carolina and Portugal, in the Years 1774 to 1776, *ed. Evangeline Walker Andrews, in collaboration with Charles McLean Andrews. New Haven: Yale University Press, 1923. Pages 141, 146–48, 153–54, 155, 158, 160–61, 180–81, 186–89, 191–94, 196, 210, 211, 212.*

2

Madame Riedesel at the Battle of Saratoga

Frederica Charlotte Louise, Baroness von Riedesel (1746–1808), was the wife of General Friedrich Adolphus Riedesel. He was in command of troops from Brunswick, Germany, hired by the British to help put down the American rebellion. When he left home, he asked his wife to join him in Quebec for what he thought would be a short campaign. Frederica thus came to America in 1777 not as a traveler but as a camp follower. She could not know that she was to remain in the New World until 1783.

WOLFENBÜTTEL, GERMANY, MARCH 8, 1776

Dearest, best Mother: . . . I could not endure the thought of separating myself from you, especially for so long a time; and yet, the thought that you begged me—nay, commanded me to remain here, made me shudder. Yet to remain, when the best, the tenderest of husbands allowed me to follow him, would have been impossible. Duty, love and conscience forbade it. It is the duty of a wife to leave all and follow her husband.

EN ROUTE TO ENGLAND, MAY 14, 1776

I still felt the greatness of my undertaking too much not to have a heavy heart, especially as my friends had not ceased to repeat to me the dangers to which I exposed myself. Gustava, my eldest daughter, was four years and nine months old; Frederica, my second, two years; and Caroline, my youngest child, just ten weeks old. I had, therefore, need of all my courage and all my tenderness to keep me from relinquishing my unprecedented wish to follow my husband. They represented to me not only the perils of the sea, but told me, also, that we were in danger of being eaten by the savages, and that the people in America lived upon horse-flesh and cats. Yet all this frightened me less than the thought of going into a country where I could not understand the language.

Frederica spent frustrating months in England waiting for a suitable ship, then joined her husband in Canada. She had put her time to good use by learning English. The family spent their first months in Quebec in winter quarters, living comfortably. When in the spring the campaign moved into New England, Frederica begged to be allowed to accompany the troops. She and several other wives were given permission to do so.

NEW YORK STATE, OCTOBER 7, 1777

I had a large calash [carriage] made for me, in which I, my children, and both my women servants had seats; and in this manner I followed the army, in the midst of the soldiers, who were merry, singing songs, and burning with a desire for victory. We passed through boundless forests and magnificent tracts of country, which, however, were abandoned by all the inhabitants, who fled before us, and reinforced the army of the American general, Gates. In the sequel this cost us dearly, for every one of them was a soldier by nature, and could shoot very well; besides, the thought of fighting for their fatherland and their freedom, inspired them with still greater courage.

During this time, my husband was obliged to encamp with the main body of the army. I remained about an hour's march behind the army, and visited my husband every morning in the camp. Very often I took my noon meal with him, but most of the time he came over to my quarters and eat [sic] with me.

The army were engaged daily in small skirmishes, but all of them of little consequence. . . .

I observed considerable movement among the troops. My husband thereupon informed me, that there was to be a reconnaissance, which, however, did not surprise me, as this often happened. On my way homeward, I met many savages in their war-dress, armed with guns. To my question where they were going, they cried out to me, "War, war!" which meant that they were going to fight.

This completely overwhelmed me, and I had scarcely got back to my quarters, when I heard skirmishing, and firing, which by degrees, became constantly heavier, until, finally, the noises became frightful. It was a terrible cannonade, and I was more dead than alive.

SARATOGA, OCTOBER 10

The whole army clamored for a retreat, and my husband promised to make it possible, provided only that no time was lost. But General [John] Burgoyne . . . could not determine upon this course, and lost every thing by his loitering.

About two o'clock in the afternoon, the firing of cannon and small arms was again heard, and all was alarm and confusion. My husband sent me a message telling me to betake myself forthwith into a house which was not far from there. I seated myself in the calash with my children, and had scarcely driven up to the house, when I saw on the opposite side of the Hudson river, five or six men with guns, which were aimed at us. Almost involuntarily I threw the children on the bottom of the calash and myself over them. At the same instant the churls fired, and shattered the arm of a poor English soldier behind us, who was already wounded, and was also on the point of retreating into the house. Immediately after our arrival a frightful cannonade began, principally directed against the house in which we had sought shelter, probably because the enemy believed, from seeing so many people flocking around it, that all the generals made it their head-quarters. Alas! It harbored none but wounded soldiers, or women!

We were finally obliged to take refuge in a cellar, in which I laid myself down in a corner not far from the door. My children laid down on the earth with their heads upon my lap, and in this manner we passed the entire night. A horrible stench, the cries of the children, and yet more than all this, my own anguish, prevented me from closing my eyes.

On the following morning the cannonade again began, but from a different side. I advised all to go out of the cellar for a little while, during which time I would have it cleaned, as otherwise we would all be sick. They followed my suggestion, and I at once set many hands to work, which was in the highest degree necessary; for the women and children being afraid to venture forth, had soiled the whole cellar.

After they had all gone out and left me alone, I for the first time surveyed our place of refuge. It consisted of three beautiful cellars, splendidly arched. I proposed that the most dangerously wounded of the officers should be brought into one of them; that the women should remain in another; and that all the rest should stay in the third, which was nearest the entrance. I had just given the cellars a good sweeping, and had fumigated them by sprinkling vinegar on burning coals, and each one had found his place prepared for him—when a fresh and terrible cannonade threw us all once more into alarm.

Many persons, who had no right to come in, threw themselves against the door. My children were already under the cellar steps, and we would all have been crushed, if God had not given me strength to place myself before the door, and with extended arms prevent all from coming in; otherwise every one of us would have been severely injured. Eleven cannon balls went through the house, and we could plainly hear them rolling over our heads. . . . In this horrible situation we remained six days. Finally, they spoke of capitulating, as by temporizing for so long a time, our retreat had been cut off. A cessation of hostilities took place.

OCTOBER 17

The capitulation was consummated. The generals waited upon the American general-in-chief, [Horatio] Gates, and the troops laid down their arms, and surrendered themselves prisoners of war.*

At last, my husband sent to me a groom with a message that I should come to him with our children. I, therefore, again seated myself in my dear calash; and in the passage through the American camp, I observed, with great satisfaction, that no one cast at us scornful glances. On the contrary, they all greeted me, even showing compassion on their countenances at seeing a mother with her little children in such a situation. I confess that I feared to come into the enemy's camp, as the thing was so entirely new to me. When I approached the tents, a noble looking man came toward me, took the children out of the wagon, embraced and kissed them, and then with tears in his eyes helped me also to alight.

"You tremble," said he to me, "fear nothing."

"No," replied I, "for you are so kind, and have been so tender toward my children, that it has inspired me with courage."†

The agreement that the troops would be sent back to England, on condition that they did not again fight against the Americans, was not, in the end, approved. Riedesel's troops remained in Boston and Cambridge until the fall of 1778, when they were ordered to Virginia.

NOVEMBER 1778

My husband, fortunately, found a pretty English wagon, and bought it for me, so that, as before, I was enabled to travel easily. My little Gustava had entreated one of my husband's adjutants, Captain Edmonston, not to leave us on the way. The confiding manner of the child touched him, and he gave his promise and faithfully kept it. I traveled always with the army, and often over almost impassable roads. The captain, who was

*General John Burgoyne surrendered six generals, 300 other officers, and almost 5000 enlisted men. The Battle of Saratoga was the turning point of the war. The American victory gave heart to many patriots and they came from all points to enlist.

†The kind American general was Philip Schuyler, who had been replaced as commander by Gates just two months earlier.

very strong and always at hand, sprang from his horse at every dangerous place, and held our wagon. Our old yäger [groom], Rockel, who was with me and was much delighted at this assistance, as he was very much fatigued, often sat quietly on his box and contented himself with crying, "Captain!" Instantly he was down from his horse. . . .

One day we came to a pretty little place, but our supply wagon not having been able to follow us, we could not endure our hunger longer. Observing a quantity of butcher's meat in the house in which we put up, I begged the hostess to let me have some.

"I have," answered she, "several different kinds. There is beef, veal, and mutton." My mouth already watered at the prospect.

"Let me have some," I said, "I will pay you well for it."

Snapping her fingers almost under my very nose, she replied, "You shall not have a morsel of it. Why have you come out of your land to kill us, and waste our goods and possessions? Now you are our prisoners; it is, therefore, our turn to torment you."

"See," rejoined I, "these poor children, they are almost dead with hunger." She remained inflexible. But when, finally, my three and a half year old little daughter, Caroline, came up to her, seized her by the hand, and said to her in English, "Good woman, I am very hungry!" She could no longer withstand her: she took her in a room and gave her an egg.

"No," said the good little child, "I have still two sisters."

At this the woman was touched, and gave her three eggs, saying, "I am just as angry as ever, but I cannot withstand the child." She then became more gentle, and offered me bread and milk. I made tea for ourselves. The woman eyed us longingly, for the Americans love it very much; but they had resolved to drink it no longer, as the famous duty on the tea had occasioned the war. I offered her a cup and poured out for her a saucer of tea. This mollified her completely.

When we arrived in Virginia, and were only a day's journey from the place of our destination, we had actually nothing more remaining but our tea, and none of us could obtain any thing but bread and butter. A countryman, whom we met on the way, gave me only a hand full of acrid fruits. At noon we came to a dwelling where I begged for something to eat. They refused me with hard words, saying that there was nothing for dogs of Royalists. Seeing some Turkish [i.e. Indian] meal lying around, I begged for a couple of hands full, that I might mix it with water and make bread. The woman answered me "No, that is for our negroes, who work for us, but you have wished to kill us."

They reached Colle in February 1779, and remained there for almost a year, when the general was exchanged for an American prisoner and given a command in New York. Frederica bore another daughter in March 1780; they named her America. In July 1781 the general was sent to Canada, where they settled at Sorell. Frederica had still another daughter, named Canada; unfortunately the child succumbed to fever after five months. In 1783, after the peace treaty was signed, the Riedesel family left America for their home in Germany.

Frederica Charlotte Louise (von Massow), Baroness von Riedesel, Letters and Journals Relating to the War of the American Revolution and the Capture of the German Troops at Saratoga, *tr. William L. Stone. Albany: Joel Munsell, 1867; reprinted, New York Times & Arno Press, 1968. Pages 36–38, 115–16, 127–29, 133–35, 145–47, 152–53. A revised translation by Marvin L. Brown, Jr., was published as* Baroness von Riedesel and the American Revolution: Journal and Correspondence of a Tour of Duty, 1776–1783. *Chapel Hill, N.C.: University of North Carolina Press, 1965.*

3

Madame de La Tour du Pin Manages a New York Farm

Henrietta-Lucy (Dillon) (1770–1853) and her husband, Frédéric-Séraphin de La Tour du Pin de Gouvernet, fled for their lives from Bordeaux during the Reign of Terror in 1794. As members of the aristocracy, they were in grave danger, and with others in their situation, they sought to escape France. When Henrietta learned that a small sailing vessel, the Diane, *had been cleared to leave Bordeaux for Boston, she persuaded the captain to take her family as passengers. The couple and their children, with a friend, M. de Chambeau, stole out of the city with what they could save of their possessions. Their fathers, as they learned later, were executed during the Terror.*

On arrival in Boston they received letters from a relative in England who put them in touch with General Philip Schuyler. He invited them to come to his home near Albany, New York, where he offered to help them find a farm. They stayed in America for two years.

ALBANY, NEW YORK, JUNE 1794

After remaining a month at Boston we set out with our two children, Humbert and Séraphine, the first of June, and fifteen days later we arrived at Albany. We traversed the whole state of Massachusetts, of which we admired the fertility and the air of prosperity.

As we did not wish to remain at Albany, General Schuyler took charge of finding us a farm which we could buy in the neighborhood. . . . My husband visited several farms. We were awaiting the arrival of the funds which had been sent us from Holland. . . . General Schuyler and Mr. Van Rensselaer advised my husband to divide his funds into three equal parts: A third for the purchase; a third for the management, the purchase of negroes, horses, cows, agricultural implements and household furniture; and a third part, added to what remained of the 12,000 francs brought by us from Bordeaux, for a reserve fund to meet unexpected circumstances, such as the loss of negroes or cattle and also for living expenses the first year. This arrangement became our rule of conduct.

Personally, I resolved to be in a position to fulfill my duties as manager of the farm. I began by accustoming myself never to remain in bed after sunrise. At three o'clock in the morning, during the summer, I was up and dressed. . . .

We had acquired moccasins, a kind of foot-covering of buffalo-skin, made and sold by the Indians. The price of these articles was sometimes quite high, when they were embroidered with dyed bark or with porcupine quills.

It was in purchasing these moccasins that I saw the Indians for the first time. They were the last survivors of the Mohawk tribe whose territory had been purchased or taken by the Americans since the peace. The Onondagas, established near Lake Champlain, also were selling their forests and disappearing at this epoch. From time to time some of them came to us. I was a little surprised when I met for the first time a man and woman practically nude promenading tranquilly upon the highway, without any one seeming to find this remarkable. But I soon became accustomed to this, and, when I was settled on the farm, I saw them almost every day during the summer.*

We took advantage of the first moment that the route was traced and trodden down to commence our moving. The funds which we awaited from Holland had arrived and my grandmother, Lady Dillon, who had died the nineteenth of June,

---

*The farm they purchased was on the Hudson River, on the road from Troy to Schenectady and four miles from Albany. They could not take possession until the cold weather, after a road had been packed down through the snow.

had left me a legacy of 300 guineas, although she had never seen me. With this money we bought our farm utensils. . . .

At this time we bought a negro, and this purchase, which seemed to be the most simple thing in the world, produced in my case a feeling so new that I shall remember it all my life.*

The house comprised only the rooms on the ground floor and was raised five feet above the earth. At the time it was built they had commenced by constructing a wall, buried six feet in the ground and rising two feet above the surface. This part formed the cellar and the milk-room. Above, the rest of the house was of wood, as you will still see frequently in Switzerland. The vacant spaces in the carpentry work were filled with sun-dried bricks which formed a wall very compact and very warm.

My butter had become very popular. I arranged it carefully in little rolls formed in a mould marked with our cipher, and placed it attractively in a very neat basket upon a fine serviette. It was for general sale. We had eight cows which were well fed, and our butter did not feel the effects of the winter. My cream was always fresh. This brought me in every day quite a little money, and the sledge-load of wood also sold for at least two dollars.

Our slave, Prime, although he did not know how to read or write, nevertheless kept his accounts with such exactitude that there was never the slightest error. He often brought back some fresh meat which he had bought at Albany, and, upon his return, my husband, from his report, wrote out the sum of the receipts and expenditures.

Property like ours was generally burdened with a small rent which was paid either in grain or in money. Our farm paid to the patroon, Van Rensselaer, twenty-two pecks of corn, either in kind or in money. All of the farms in his immense estate, which was eighteen miles wide by forty-two miles long, were held under the same conditions.†

---

*New York State passed an emancipation law in 1828. Before that time "free negroes" in the North were local slaves who had been freed by their owners. If these could not be hired, farmers purchased slaves.

†The Van Rensselaer family had held the proprietorship of Rensselaer-

The Indians, who had not appeared during the entire winter, began to visit the farms. One of them, at the beginning of the cold weather, had asked my permission to cut some branches of a kind of willow tree which had shoots, large as my thumb and five or six feet long. He promised me to weave some baskets during the winter season. I counted little upon this promise, as I did not believe that Indians would keep their word to this degree, although I had been so informed.

I was mistaken. Within a week after the snow had melted, my Indian came back with a load of baskets. He gave me six of them which were nested in one another. The first, which was round and very large, was so well made that, when filled with water, it retained it like an earthen vessel. I wished to pay him for the baskets, but he absolutely refused and would accept only a bowl of buttermilk of which the Indians are very fond.

A nice wagon, loaded with fine vegetables, often passed before our door. It belonged to the Shakers, who were located at a distance of six or seven miles. The driver of the wagon always stopped at our house, and I never failed to talk with him about their manner of life, their customs, and their belief. He urged us to visit their establishment, and we decided to go there some day. It is known that this sect of Quakers belonged to the reformed school of the original Quakers who took refuge in America with Penn.

After the war of 1763, an English woman [Ann Lee] set herself up for a reformer apostle. She made many proselytes in the states of Vermont and Massachusetts. Several families put their property in common and bought land in the then uninhabited parts of the country, but, as the clearings approached and reached them, they sold their establishment in order to retire further into the wilderness.

Those of whom I speak were then protected on all sides by a forest several miles deep. They therefore had no reason as yet to fear their neighbors. Their establishment was bounded on

---

swyck since the seventeenth century. General Schuyler's wife was Catherine Van Rensselaer, and one of their daughters also married into the family.

one side by woods which covered 20,000 acres, belonging to the city of Albany, and on the other by the river Mohawk. . . .

Our negro, Prime, who knew all the routes in our neighborhood, conducted us to their place. At the start we were at least three hours in the woods, following a road which was hardly laid out. Then after having passed the barriers which marked the limits of the Shaker property, the road became more distinct and better marked. But we still had to pass through a very thick forest, broken here and there by fields where cows and horses were pastured at liberty. Finally, we came out in a vast clearing traversed by a pretty stream and surrounded on all sides by woods. In the midst was erected the establishment, composed of a large number of nice wooden houses, a church, schools, and a community house of brick. . . .

Everything was in a state of the greatest prosperity, but without the least evidence of elegance. Many men and women were working at the cultivation or the weeding of the garden. The sale of vegetables represented the principal source of revenue to the community.

We visited the schools for the boys and girls, the immense community stables, the dairies, and the factories in which they produced the butter and cheese. . . .

[At a prayer meeting] I was seated at the corner of the chimney, and my guide had enjoined silence, which was all the easier for me as I was alone. While keeping absolutely silent, I had the opportunity to admire the floor, which was constructed of pine wood, without any knots, and of a rare perfection and whiteness. Upon this fine floor were drawn in different directions lines represented by copper nails, brilliantly polished, the heads of which were level with the floor. I endeavored to divine what could be the use of these lines, which did not seem to have any connection with each other, when at the last stroke of the bell the two side doors opened, and I saw enter on my side fifty or sixty young girls or women, preceded by one who was older who seated herself upon one of the arm-chairs. No child accompanied them.

The men were arranged in the same manner at the opposite side, where were my husband and Monsieur de Chambeau. I then observed that the women stood upon these lines of nails, taking care not to cross them with their toes. They remained immobile until the moment when the woman seated in the arm-chair gave a sort of groan or cry which was neither speech nor song. All then changed their places, and I imagined that this kind of stifled cry which I had heard must represent some command. After several evolutions, they stopped, and the old woman murmured quite a long string of words in a language which was absolutely unintelligible, but in which were mingled, it seemed to me, some English words. After this, they went out in the same order in which they had entered. Having thus visited all parts of the establishment, we took leave of our kind guide and entered our wagon to return home, very little edified regarding the hospitality of the Shakers.

One thing had rendered me at once very popular with my neighbors. The day that we took possession of our farm, I adopted the costume worn by the women on the neighboring places, that is to say, a skirt of blue and black striped wool, a little camisole of light brown cotton cloth, a handkerchief of the same color, with my hair parted as it is worn now, and caught up with a comb. In winter, I wore gray or blue woolen stockings, with moccasins or slippers of buffalo skin; in summer, cotton stockings, and shoes. I never put on a dress or a corset, except to go into the city.

Among the effects which I had brought to America were two or three riding-costumes. These I used to transform myself into a *dame élégante,* when I wished to pay a visit to the Schuylers or Van Rensselaers, for very frequently we dined and afterwards passed the evening with them, particularly when it was moonlight, and above all, during the period of snow.

Tragedy struck the family when little Séraphine died of infantile paralysis. A little son of the Schuylers who had been playing with the child also died within a few hours.

Although all joy had disappeared from our household, it was none the less necessary for us to continue our work, and we encouraged each other, my husband and I, to find distraction in the obligation under which we were not to remain a moment idle.

The harvest of the apples approached. It promised to be very abundant, for our orchard had the finest appearance. We could count upon the trees as many apples as there were leaves. The autumn before we had essayed what is known at Bordeaux as *une façon*. This consists in turning over with a spade a square of four or five feet around each tree, something which had never been done there before. The Americans indeed have no idea of the effect which that produces upon vegetation; but when, in the springtime, they saw our trees covered with blossoms, they looked upon us as sorcerers.

Another act brought us great reputation. Instead of buying for our cider new barrels made of very porous wood, we succeeded in finding at Albany several casks which had contained Bordeaux and also some marked *cognac* which were well known to us. Then we arranged our cellar with the same care as if it were to contain wine of the Médoc [wine district]. We borrowed a cider mill to crush the apples. A horse twenty-three years old which General Schuyler had given me was hitched to it. . . . The horse had carried him through the war. . . .

Our reputation for honesty was so great that people had confidence that we would not put any water into our cider. This enabled us to sell it at double the ordinary price, and all was sold at once.

The crop of corn followed that of the apples. This crop was very abundant as it is the one that succeeds best in the United States where it is indigenous. As you must not leave the ear covered with the husk more than two days, we brought together all of our neighbors to finish the harvest quickly on the spot. This is what is called a "husking bee." We began by sweeping the floor of the barn with as much care as though we were going to give a ball. Then when night arrived, we lighted several candles and the people assembled, about thirty in all, black and white, and set themselves to work. One of the party did not cease to sing or to tell stories. Towards the middle of the night we served to each one a bowl of hot milk which we had previously mixed with cider. To this mixture you add five or six pounds of brown sugar, if you are prodigal, or an equal amount of molasses, if you are not, then spices, such as cloves, cinnamon and nutmeg. Our workers drank to our very best health the contents of an immense washboiler filled with this mixture, with which they ate toast.

Early in 1796, letters came from France informing the couple that they would have to return home to protect their property.

These dispatches fell in the midst of our tranquil occupations like a fire-brand which quickly lighted in the hearts of all around me the thought of a return to their native land. As for myself, I had an entirely different feeling. France had left in my mind only a recollection of horror. . . . A sort of presentiment caused me to foresee that I was going to encounter a new life of trouble and anxieties. My husband did not dream of the intensity of my regret when I saw the moment of our departure arrive. I imposed only one condition, that of giving our slaves their liberty. My husband consented and reserved for me alone this happiness.

These poor people, on seeing the letters arrive from Europe, had feared some change in our life. They were disturbed and alarmed. Therefore, all four of them were trembling when they entered my room to which I had called them. They found me alone. I said to them with emotion: "My friends, we are going to return to Europe. What shall I do with you?"

The poor creatures were overcome. Judith dropped into a chair, in tears, while the three men covered their faces with their hands, and all remained silent.

I continued: "We have been so satisfied with you that it is just that you should be recompensed. My husband has charged me to tell you that he will give you your liberty."

On hearing this word our good servants were so stupified that they remained for several seconds without speech. Then all four threw themselves at my feet crying: "Is it possible? Do you mean that we are free?"

I replied: "Yes, upon my honor, from this moment, as free as I am myself."

Who can describe the poignant emotion of such a moment! Never in my life had I experienced anything so sweet. Those whom I had just promised their liberty surrounded me in tears. They kissed my hand, my feet, my dress, and then suddenly their joy ceased and they said: "We would prefer to remain slaves all our lives, if you will stay here."

The following day my husband took them to Albany before a judge, for the ceremony of the *manumission*, an act which had to be public. All the negroes of the city were present. The Justice of the Peace, who was at the same time the steward of Mr. Van Rensselaer, was in very bad humor. He attempted to assert that Prime, being fifty years of age, could not under the terms of the law be given his liberty unless he was assured a pension of a hundred dollars. But Prime had foreseen this case, and he produced his certificate of baptism which attested that he was only forty-nine. They made the slaves kneel before my husband, and he placed his hand upon the head of each to sanction his liberation, exactly in the manner of ancient Rome.

Nothing in the education or experience of either Henrietta or her husband had prepared them for farm life. She was brought up in a home of extravagant wealth, the granddaughter of the corrupt archbishop of Narbonne. She was an attendant of Queen Marie Antoinette in Versailles. She had always been waited upon by servants. Her family, the Dillons, were English, and she, of course, spoke English well, but the count spoke it imperfectly. She had reason to be proud of their success as farmers.

The Count and Countess de La Tour du Pin returned to France but remained only a short time when they were forced to leave again, this time for England. In 1800 they were repatriated. The count represented France under Napoleon at the Hague, then served, until his death in 1837, under Louis XVIII. He had been made a peer and given the title of Marquis. In 1820 Madame de La Tour du Pin began writing her Journal d'une Femme de Cinquante Ans. *Their American adventures occupy a section of the book, which was published by her great grandson in 1906.*

Henrietta-Lucy (Dillon), Marquise de La Tour du Pin de Gauvernet, Recollections of the Revolution and the Empire, from the French of the "Journal d'une Femme de Cinqante Ans" by la Marquise de la Tour du Pin, *ed. and tr. Walter Geer. New York: Brentano, 1920. Pages 189, 196–97, 207–219, 230–33, 238–40.*

4

Fanny Wright's Reasoned View of Democracy

*Two Englishwomen, Frances Wright (1795–1852) and her sister Ca-
milla, arrived in the United States in September, 1818, occasioning
comment because of their beauty and youth (they were respectively 23
and 21), and also because they were traveling without an escort. Their
parents died when both girls were infants and they grew up in
comparative freedom in the homes of relatives. They spent almost two
years in America (1818–1820), returning later, in 1824. From that
date much of Fanny's life was spent in the United States.*

WHITEHOUSE, NEW JERSEY, DECEMBER 1819

It has been common of late years to summon the literature of
America to the European bar and to pass a verdict against
American wit and American science. More liberal foreigners,
in alluding to the paucity of standing American works in prose
or rhyme, are wont to ascribe it to the infant state of society in
this country; others read this explanation, I incline to think at
least, without affixing a just meaning to the words. Is it not
commonly received in England that the American nation is in
a sort of middle state between barbarism and refinement?

I remember that, on coming to this country, I had myself
but a very confused notion of the people that I was to find in
it. Sometimes they had been depicted to me as a tribe of wild
colts, chewing the bit just put into their mouths and fretting

26

under the curb of law, carelessly administered and yet too strict withal for their untamed spirits; at other times I understood them to be a race of shrewd artificers, speculating merchants, and plodding farmers, with just enough of manners to growl an answer when questioned and enough of learning to read a newspaper, drive a hard bargain, keep accounts, and reason phlegmatically upon the advantages of free trade and popular government. These portraits appeared to me to have few features of resemblance—the one seemed nearly to image out a Dutchman and the other a wild Arab. To conceive the two characters combined were not very possible; I looked at both and could make nothing of either.

The history of this people seemed to declare that they were brave, high-minded, and animated with the soul of liberty; their institutions, that they were enlightened; their laws, that they were humane; and their policy, that they were peaceful, and kept good faith. But I was told that they were none of these. Judge a man by his works, it is said, but to judge a nation by its works was no adage, and, I was taught, was quite ridiculous. To judge a nation by the reports of its enemies, however, seemed equally ridiculous, so I determined not to judge at all, but to land in the country without knowing anything about it and wait until it should speak for itself.

The impressions that I have received, I have occasionally attempted to impart to you; they were such at first as greatly to surprise me, for it is scarcely possible to keep the mind unbiased by current reports, however contradictory their nature and however intent we may be to let them pass unheeded.

There is little here that bespeaks the infancy of society in the sense that foreigners usually suppose it applicable. The simple morals, more equalized fortunes, and more domestic habits and attachments, generally found in this country as compared with Europe, doubtless bespeak a nation young in luxury, but do they bespeak a nation young in knowledge? It would say little for knowledge were this the case.

It is true that authorship is not yet a trade in this country. Perhaps for the poor it is a poor trade everywhere, and could men do better, they might seldom take to it as a profession.

But, however this may be, many causes have operated hitherto, and some perhaps may always continue to operate, to prevent American genius from showing itself in works of imagination or of arduous literary labour. As yet, we must remember that the country itself is not half a century old. The generation is barely passed away whose energies were engrossed by a struggle for existence. To the harassing war of the Revolution succeeded the labors of establishing the national government and of reorganizing that of the several states, and it must be remembered that, in America, neither war nor legislation is the occupation of a body of men, but of the whole community; it occupies every head and every heart, rouses the whole energy, and absorbs the whole genius of the nation.

The establishment of the federal government was not the work of a day; even after its conception and adoption a thousand clashing opinions were to be combated. The war of the pen succeeded to that of the sword, and the shock of political parties to that of hostile armies; the struggle continued through the whole of that administration denominated *Federal*. After the election of Mr. Jefferson, it revived for a moment with redoubled violence, and though this was but the flickering of the flame in the socket, it engaged the attention of the whole people and continued to do so until the breaking out of the second war [1812], which, in its progress, cemented all parties and, in its issue, established the national independence and perfected the civil union. It is but four years, therefore, that the public mind has been at rest; nay, it is only so long that the United States can be said to have enjoyed an acknowledged national existence.

NEW YORK, FEBRUARY 1820

The fact is that every sapient prophecy with regard to America has been disproved. We were forewarned that she was too free, and her liberty has proved her security; too peaceable, and she has been found sufficient for her defence; too large, and her size has ensured her union. These numerous republics, scattered through so wide a range of territory, embracing all the climates and containing all the various products of the earth, seem destined, in the course of years, to form a world within themselves, independent alike of the treasures and the industry of all the other sections of the globe. Each year they are learning, more and more, to look to each other for all the various articles of food and raiment, while the third great human necessity, defence, they have been from infancy practised to furnish in common. The bonds of union, indeed, are more numerous and intimate than can be easily conceived by foreigners. A people who have bled together for liberty, who equally appreciate and equally enjoy that liberty which their own blood or that of their fathers has purchased, who feel, too, that the liberty which they love has found her last asylum on their shores—such a people are bound together by ties of amity and citizenship far beyond what is usual in national communities.

WASHINGTON, APRIL 1820

My personal observation has been confined to a portion of this vast country, the whole of whose surface merits the study of a more discerning traveller than myself. I own that as regards the southern states I have ever felt a secret reluctance to visit their territory. The sight of slavery is revolting everywhere, but to inhale the impure breath of its pestilence in the free winds of America is odious beyond all that the imagination can conceive. I do not mean to indulge in idle declamation either against the injustice of the masters or upon the degradation of the slave. This is a subject upon which it is difficult to reason, because it is so easy to feel.

The difficulties that stand in the way of emancipation, I can perceive to be numerous; but should the masters content themselves with idly deploring the evil, instead of "setting their shoulder to the wheel" and actively working out its remedy, neither their courtesy in the drawing room, their virtues in domestic life, nor even their public services in the senate and the field will preserve the southern planters from the reprobation of their northern brethren, and the scorn of mankind.

The Virginians are said to pride themselves upon the peculiar tenderness with which they visit the sceptre of authority upon their African vassals. As all those acquainted with the character of the Virginia planters, whether Americans or foreigners, appear to concur in bearing testimony to their humanity, it is probable that they are entitled to the praise which they claim. But in their position, justice should be held superior to humanity; to break the chains would be more generous than to gild them, and, whether we consider the interests of the master or the slave, decidedly more useful.

It is true that this neither can nor ought to be done too hastily. To give liberty to a slave before he understands its value is, perhaps, rather to impose a penalty than to bestow a blessing; but it is not clear to me that the southern planters are duly exerting themselves to prepare the way for that change in the condition of their black population which they profess to think not only desirable but inevitable.

From the conversations of some distinguished Virginians, I cannot but apprehend that they suffer themselves to be disheartened by the slender success which has hitherto attended the exertions of those philanthropists who have made the character and condition of the negro their study and care. . . .

Why does not Virginia recur to the plan marked out by herself in the first year of her independence? Has she not virtue to execute what she had wisdom to conceive? She has made so many noble sacrifices to humanity and patriotism, her history records so many acts of heroism and disinterested generosity, that I am willing to persuade myself she is equal to this also. Nor can she be so blind to the future as not to perceive the consequences with which she is threatened, should she not take some active measures to eradicate the Egyptian plague which covers her soil. A servile war is the least of the evils which could befall her; the ruin of her moral character, the decay of her strength, the loss of her political importance, vice, indolence, degradation—these are the evils that will overtake her.

A few years later, Fanny herself "put her shoulder to the wheel" and established at Nashoba, in Tennessee, a colony where the children of slaves were to be educated equally with white children, to prove that black skin did not make an inferior race. Frances Trollope speaks of the colony (see below, p. 33), which she saw in 1828 when its failure seemed certain. Poor health forced Fanny and her sister Camilla to leave Nashoba, and the colony was judged a failure. Later Fanny took her slaves to Haiti, where they were given freedom. She remained in the United States for some time, writing and lecturing. Her radical views on education, religion, and the oppression of women, as well as her audacity in speaking in public, made her notorious. In 1831 she married Phiquepal D'Arusmont, a marriage that soon ended in divorce. She spent her last years in the United States and resumed her career as a lecturer. She died in Cincinnati in 1852.

Frances Wright (later D'Arusmont), Views of Society and Manners in America. *London: Longman, Hurst, Rees, Orme and Brown, 1821. Pages 162–64, 208, 267–70.*

5

Frances Trollope Did Not Love Us

Frances Trollope (1780–1863) came to the United States in 1827 to establish herself in business, with the expectation that her eldest son would eventually be able to manage it and thus help the family out of its financial difficulties. She brought with her three of her children and a manservant, leaving at home her husband, a lawyer with a failing practice, and the two older sons, still at school.

Accompanying her were Auguste Hervieu, a young French artist, and Fanny Wright, the wealthy English radical who was returning to Nashoba, the experimental colony she had founded in Tennessee (see pages 30–31).

Mrs. Trollope spent three years in America.

NEW ORLEANS, DECEMBER 1827

On first touching the soil of a new land, of a new continent, of a new world, it is impossible not to feel considerable excitement and deep interest in almost every object that meets us. New-Orleans presents very little that can gratify the eye of taste, but nevertheless there is much of novelty and interest for a newly-arrived European. The large proportion of blacks seen in the streets, all labour being performed by them; the grace and beauty of the elegant Quadroons; the occasional groups of wild and savage looking Indians; the unwonted aspect of the vege-tation; the huge and turbid river, with its low and slimy shore, all help to afford that species of amusement which proceeds from looking at what we never saw before.

Miss Wright, then less known (though the author of more than one clever volume) than she has since become, was the companion of our voyage from Europe; and it was my purpose to have passed some months with her and her sister at the estate she had purchased in Tennessee. This lady, since become so celebrated as the advocate of opinions that make millions shudder, and some half-score admire, was, at the time of my leaving England with her, dedicated to a pursuit widely different from her subsequent occupations. Instead of becoming a public orator in every town throughout America, she was about, as she said, to seclude herself for life in the deepest forest of the western world, that her fortune, her time, and her talents might be exclusively devoted to aid the cause of the suffering Africans.

Her first object was to show that nature had made no difference between blacks and whites, excepting in complexion; and this she expected to prove by giving an education perfectly equal to a class of black and white children. Could this fact be once fully established she conceived that the Negro cause would stand on firmer ground than it had yet done, and the degraded rank which they have ever held among civilized nations would be proved to be a gross injustice.

This question of the mental equality or inequality between us and the Negro race, is one of great interest, and has certainly never yet been fairly tried; and I expected for my children and myself both pleasure and information from visiting her establishment, and watching the success of her experiment.

Mrs. Trollope arrived at Nashoba after an uncomfortable trip up the "dismal" Mississippi River by steamboat and then through a roadless forest in a "Deerborn" carriage.

One glance sufficed to convince me that every idea I had formed of the place was as far as possible from the truth. Desolation was the only feeling—the only word that presented itself; but it was not spoken. I think, however, that Miss Wright was aware of the painful impression the sight of her forest home produced on me, and I doubt not that the conviction reached us both at the same moment, that we had erred in thinking that a few months passed together at this spot could be productive of pleasure to either. . . . I decided upon leaving the place with as little delay as possible, and did so at the end of ten days.

Mrs. Trollope and her entourage proceeded to Cincinnati, which had been recommended to her as a place favorable to the establishment of a bazaar for the sale of European goods. While the bazaar was being built for her in the city, she rented a cottage in a nearby community.

Mohawk, as our little village was called, gave us an excellent opportunity of comparing the peasants of the United States with those of England, and of judging the average degree of comfort enjoyed by each. I believe Ohio gives as fair a specimen as any part of the Union; if they have the roughness and inconveniences of a new state to contend with, they have higher wages and cheaper provisions; if I err in supposing it a mean state in point of comfort, it certainly is not taking too low a standard.

Mechanics, if good workmen, are certain of employment, and good wages, rather higher than with us; the average wages of a labourer throughout the Union is ten dollars a month, with lodging, boarding, washing, and mending; if he lives at his own expense he has a dollar a day. It appears to me that the necessaries of life, that is to say, meat, bread, butter, tea, and coffee (not to mention whiskey), are within the reach of every sober, industrious, and healthy man who chooses to have them; and yet I think that an English peasant, with the same qualifications, would, in coming to the United States, change for the worse. He would find wages somewhat higher, and provisions in western America considerably lower; but this statement, true as it is, can lead to nothing but delusion if taken apart from other facts, fully as certain, and not less important, but which require more detail in describing, and which perhaps cannot be fully comprehended, except by an eyewitness.

The American poor are accustomed to eat meat three times a day; I never inquired into the habits of any cottagers in western America, where this was not the case. . . . Ardent spirits, though lamentably cheap, still cost something, and the use of them among the men, with more or less of discretion, according to the character, is universal. Tobacco also grows at their doors, and is not taxed: yet this too costs something, and the air of heaven is not in more general use among the men of America than chewing tobacco. I am not now pointing out the evils of dram-drinking, but it is evident, that where this practice prevails universally, and often to the most frightful excess, the consequence must be, that the money spent to obtain the dram is less than the money lost by the time consumed in drinking it.

Long, disabling, and expensive fits of sickness are incontestibly more frequent in every part of America than in England, and the sufferers have no aid to look to, but what they have saved, or what they may be enabled to sell. I have never seen misery exceed what I have witnessed in an American cottage where disease has entered.

But if the condition of the labourer be not superior to that of the English peasant, that of his wife and daughters is incomparably worse. It is they who are indeed the slaves of the soil. One has but to look at the wife of an American cottager, and ask her age, to be convinced that the life she leads is one of hardship, privation, and labour. It is rare to see a woman in this station who has reached the age of thirty, without losing every trace of youth and beauty. You continually see women with infants on their knee, that you feel sure are their grand-children, till some convincing proof of the contrary is displayed.

Even the young girls, though often with lovely features, look pale, thin, and haggard. I do not remember to have seen in any single instance among the poor, a specimen of the plump, rosy, laughing physiognomy so common among our cottage girls. The horror of domestic service, which the reality of slavery, and the fable of equality, have generated, excludes the young women from that sure and most comfortable resource of decent English girls; and the consequence is, that with a most irreverend freedom of manner to the parents, the daughters are, to the full extent of the word, domestic slaves. . . .

They marry very young; in fact, in no rank of life do you meet with young women in that delightful period of existence between childhood and marriage, wherein, if only tolerably well spent, so much useful information is gained, and the character takes a sufficient degree of firmness to support with dignity the more important parts of wife and mother. . . .

The absence of poor-laws is, without doubt, a blessing to the country, but they have not that natural and reasonable dependence on the richer classes which, in countries differently constituted, may so well supply their place. I suppose there is less alms-giving in America than in any other Christian country on the face of the globe. It is not in the temper of the people either to give or to receive.

Mrs. Trollope was herself feeling the pinch of poverty. The bazaar was not a success. Americans did not buy the fancy good she stocked. Mr. Trollope, who was to send her funds and follow her later, dawdled for months before he arrived. Only Auguste Hervieu's drawings and teaching skills saved the household from going hungry. After a difficult two years, the Trollopes left Cincinnati. Mrs. Trollope spent another year and a half observing American society.

We were at Washington at the time that the measure for chasing the last several tribes of Indians from their forest homes, was canvassed in Congress, and finally decided upon by the *fiat* of the president. If the American character may be judged by their conduct in this matter, they are most lamentably deficient in every feeling of honour and integrity. It is among themselves, and from themselves, that I have heard the statements which represent them as treacherous and false almost beyond belief, in their intercourse with the unhappy Indians.

Had I, during my residence in the United States, observed any single feature in their national character that could justify their eternal boast of liberality and the love of freedom, I might have respected them, however much my taste might have been offended by what was peculiar in their manners and customs. But it is impossible for any mind of common honesty not to be revolted by the contradictions in their principles and practice. They inveigh against the governments of Europe, because, as they say, they favour the powerful and oppress the weak. You may hear this declaimed upon in Congress, roared out in taverns, discussed in every drawing-room, satirized upon the stage, nay, even anathematized from the pulpit: listen to it, and then look at them at home; you will see them with one hand hoisting the cap of liberty, and with the other flogging their slaves. You will see them one hour lecturing their mob on the indefeasible rights of man, and the next driving from their homes the children of the soil, whom they have bound them- selves to protect by the most solemn treaties.

Mrs. Trollope did like some things about America, principally its natural beauties, and she made some friends. But as she departed the country in 1831 she delivered her final verdict.

I speak not of my friends, nor of my friends' friends. The small patrician band is a race apart; they live with each other, and for each other. . . . I speak not of these, but of the population generally, as seen in town and country, among the rich and the poor, in the slave states and the free states. I do not like them. I do not like their principles, I do not like their manners, I do not like their opinions.

Both as a woman and as a stranger, it might be unseemly for me to say that I do not like their government, and therefore I will not say so. That it is one which pleases themselves is most certain, and this is considerably more important than pleasing all the travelling old ladies in the world. I entered the country at New-Orleans, remained for more than two years west of the Alleghanies, and passed another year among the Atlantic cities, and the country around them. I conversed during this time with citizens of all orders and degrees, and I never heard from any one a single disparaging word against their government. It is not, therefore, surprising, that when the people of that country hear strangers questioning the wisdom of their institutions, and expressing disapprobation at some of their effects, they should set it down either to an incapacity of judging, or to a malicious feeling of envy and ill-will.

"How can any one in their senses doubt the excellence of a government which we have tried for half a century, and loved the better the longer we have known it?"

Such is the natural inquiry of every American when the excellence of their government is doubted; and I am inclined to answer, that no one in their senses, who has visited the country, and known the people, can doubt its fitness for them, such as they now are, or its utter unfitness for any other people.

Fanny Trollope's book on America was not well received by American readers. Her acid comments and some similarly critical made by Charles Dickens (despite some truth in both), made Americans wary of later English visitors. But for Mrs. Trollope, the book was the first in a series of publications that made her reputation and her fortune. Her son, Anthony Trollope, became a famous novelist.

Frances Trollope, Domestic Manners of the Americans. *New York: Whittaker, Treacher, & Co., 1832. Pages 28, 33–34, 44–45, 104–107, 180, 321–22.*

6

Harriet Martineau Visits the South and Is Threatened in Boston

Harriet Martineau (1802–1876), a single woman dependent on her own earnings, began to write articles and tales while quite young. Just before her visit to the United States she completed Illustrations of Taxation, *which followed a work of nine volumes entitled* Illustrations of Political Economy, *both consisting of stories explaining these difficult subjects to laymen. When she came to the United States in 1834 she had won an international reputation as a scholarly writer. Moreover, she knew many Americans by reputation and correspondence. She was a Unitarian and an abolitionist.*

At the close of a long work which I completed in 1834, it was thought desirable that I should travel for two years. I determined to go to the United States, chiefly because I felt a strong curiosity to witness the actual working of republican institutions; and partly because the circumstance of the language being the same as my own is very important to one who, like myself, is too deaf to enjoy anything like an average opportunity of obtaining correct knowledge, where intercourse is carried on in a foreign language. I went with a mind, I believe, as nearly as possible unprejudiced about America, with a strong disposition to admire democratic institutions, but an entire ignorance how far the people of the United States lived up to, or fell below, their own theory.

I have seen much more of domestic life than could possibly have been exhibited to any gentleman travelling through the country. The nursery, the boudoir, the kitchen, are all excellent schools in which to learn the morals and manners of a people. . . . I carry [an ear] trumpet of remarkable fidelity; an instrument, moreover, which seems to exert some winning power, by which I gain more in *téte-à-tétes* than is given to people who hear general conversation.

One consequence, mournful and injurious, of the "chivalrous" taste and temper of a country with regard to its women is that it is difficult, where it is not impossible, for women to earn their bread. Where it is a boast that women do not labour, the encouragement and rewards of labour are not provided. It is so in America. In some parts, there are now so many women dependent on their own exertions for a maintenance, that the evil will give way before the force of circumstances. In the meantime, the lot of poor women is sad.

Before the opening of the factories, there were but three resources; teaching, needle-work, and keeping boarding-houses or hotels. Now, there are the mills; and women are employed in printing-offices; as compositors, as well as folders and stitchers.

The progression or emancipation of any class usually, if not always, takes place through the efforts of individuals of that class: and so it must be here. All women should inform themselves of the condition of their sex, and of their own position. It must necessarily follow that the noblest of them will, sooner or later, put forth a moral power which shall prostrate cant, and burst asunder the bonds, (silken to some, but cold iron to others,) of feudal prejudices and usages.

In the meantime, is it to be understood that the principles of the Declaration of Independence bear no relation to half of the human race? If so, what is the ground of the limitation? If not so, how is the restricted and dependent state of women to be reconciled with the proclamation that "all are endowed by their Creator with certain inalienable rights; that among these are life, liberty, and the pursuit of happiness?"

CINCINNATI

The Cincinnati public was pouring into Mrs. Trollope's bazar, to the first concert ever offered to them. This bazar is the great deformity of the city. Happily, it is not very conspicuous, being squatted down among houses nearly as lofty as the summit of its dome. From my window at the boarding-house, however, it was only too distinctly visible. It is built of brick, and has Gothic windows, Grecian pillars, and a Turkish dome, and it was originally ornamented with Egyptian devices, which have, however, all disappeared under the brush of the whitewasher.

The concert was held in a large plain room, where a quiet, well-mannered audience was collected. There was something extremely interesting in the spectacle of the first public introduction of music into this rising city. . . . The thought came across me how far we were from the musical regions of the Old World, and how lately this place had been a canebrake, echoing with the bellow and growl of wild beast; and here was the spirit of Mozart swaying and inspiring a silent crowd as if they were assembled in the chapel at Salzburg!

From the day of my entering the States till that of my leaving Philadelphia I had seen society basking in one bright sunshine of good-will. The sweet temper and kindly manners of the Americans are so striking to foreigners, that it is some time before the dazzled stranger perceives that, genuine as is all this good, evils as black as night exist along with it. I had been received with such hearty hospitality everywhere, and had lived among friends so conscientious in their regard for human rights, that, though I had heard of abolition riots, and had observed somewhat of the degradation of the blacks, my mind had not yet been really troubled about the enmity of the races.

The time of awakening must come. It began just before I left Philadelphia. . . .

The day before I left Philadelphia my old shipmate, the Prussian physician, arrived there, and lost no time in calling to tell me, with much agitation, that I must not go a step farther south; that he had heard on all hands, within two hours of his arrival, that I was an amalgamationist [i.e., she saw nothing to prevent mixed marriages], and that my having published a story against slavery would be fatal to me in the slave states.

I did not give much credit to the latter part of this news, and saw plainly that all I had to do was to go straight on. I really desired to see the working of the slave system, and was glad that my having published against its principles divested me altogether of the character of a spy, and gave me an unquestioned liberty to publish the results of what I might observe. In order to see things as they were, it was necessary that people's minds should not be prepossessed by my friends as to my opinions and conduct; and I therefore forbade my Philadelphia friends to publish in the newspapers, as they wished, an antidote to the charges already current against me.

The next day I first set foot in a slave state, arriving in the evening at Baltimore. I dreaded inexpressibly the first sight of a slave, and could not help speculating on the lot of every person of colour I saw from the windows the first few days. The servants in the house where I was were free blacks.

Before a week was over I perceived that all that is said in England of the hatred of the whites to the blacks in America is short of the truth. The slanders that I heard of the free blacks were too gross to injure my estimation of any but those who spoke them.

In Baltimore the bodies of coloured people exclusively are taken for dissection, "because the whites do not like it, and the coloured people cannot resist." It is wonderful that the bodily structure can be (with the exception of the colouring of the skin) thus assumed to be the pattern of that of the whites; that the exquisite nervous system, the instrument of moral as well as physical pleasures and pains, can be nicely investigated, on the ground of its being analogous with that of the whites; that not only the mechanism, but the sensibilities of the degraded race should be argued from to those of the exalted order, and that men come from such a study with contempt for these brethren in their countenances, hatred in their hearts, and insult on their tongues. These students are the men who cannot say that the coloured people have not nerves that quiver under moral injury, nor a brain that is on fire with insult, nor pulses that throb under oppression. These are the men who should stay the hand of the rash and ignorant possessors of power, who crush the being of creatures, like themselves, "fearfully and wonderfully made." But to speak the right word, to hold out the helping hand, these searchers into man have not light nor strength. . . .

I was glad it was over for once; but I never lost the painful feeling caused to a stranger by intercourse with slaves. No familiarity with them, no mirth or contentment on their part, ever soothed the miserable restlessness caused by the presence of a deeply-injured fellow-being. No wonder or ridicule on the spot avails anything to the stranger. He suffers, and must suffer from this, deeply and long, as surely as he is human and hates oppression.

At Baltimore and Washington again I was warned, in various stealthy ways, of perils awaiting me in the South. I had no means of ascertaining the justness of these warnings but by going on, and turning back for such vague reasons was not to be thought of. So I determined to say no word to my companions (who were in no danger), but to see the truth for myself. The threats proved idle, as I suspected they would. Throughout the South I met with very candid and kind treatment. I mention these warnings partly because they are a fact connected with the state of the country, and partly because it will afterward appear that the stranger's real danger lies in the North and West, over which the South had, in my case, greatly the advantage in liberality.

BOSTON

Dr. [William Ellery] Channing lives surrounded by the aristocracy of Boston, and by the most eminent of the clergy of his own denomination, whose lips are rarely opened on the question except to blame or ridicule the abolitionists. The whole matter was, at that time, considered "a low subject," and one not likely, therefore, to reach his ears. . . . He broke through all these temptations to silence the moment his convictions were settled; I mean not his convictions of the guilt and evil of slavery, but of its being his duty to utter his voice against it. From his peaceful and honoured retirement he came out into the storm, which might, and probably would, be fatal to his reputation, his influence, his repose, and perhaps, to more blessings than even these. . . .

When I was staying in his house at the end of the winter, I was one morning sealing up my papers in his presence, in order to their being put in a place of safety, news having reached us the night before of a design to Lynch me in the West, where I had been about to take a journey. While I was sealing, Dr. Channing told me that he hoped I should, on my return to England, boldly expose the fact that I was not allowed the liberty of going where I would in the United States. I told him I should not, while there was the far stronger fact that the natives of the country were not allowed to use this their constitutional liberty. Dr. Channing could not, at that time, have set his foot within the boundaries of half the states without danger to his life.

Miss Martineau was invited to speak to the women of the Anti-Slavery Society. She did so, declaring her agreement with the principles of the abolitionists.

Of the consequences of this simple affair it is not my intention to give any account, chiefly because it would be impossible to convey to my English readers my conviction of the smallness of the portion of American society which was concerned in the treatment inflicted upon me. The hubbub was so great, and the modes of insult were so various, as to justify distant observers in concluding that the whole nation had risen against me. I soon found how few can make a great noise, while the many are careless or ignorant of what is going on about a person or party with whom they have nothing to do.

ON THE MISSISSIPPI RIVER

No object was more striking than the canoes which we frequently saw, looking fearfully light and frail amid the strong current. The rower used a spoon-shaped paddle, and advanced with amazing swiftness; sometimes crossing before our bows, sometimes darting along under the bank, sometimes shooting across a track of moonlight. Very often there was only one person in the canoe, as in the instance I have elsewhere mentioned of a woman who was supposed to be going on a visit twenty or thirty miles up the stream. I could hardly have conceived of a solitude so intense as this appeared to me, the being alone on that rushing sea of waters, shut in by untrodden forests; the slow fishhawk wheeling overhead, and perilous masses of driftwood whirling down the current; trunks obviously uprooted by the forces of nature, and not laid low by the hand of man. What a spectacle must our boat, with its gay crowds, have appeared to such a solitary! what a revelation that there was a busy world still stirring somewhere; a fact which, I think, I should soon discredit if I lived in the depths of this wilderness, for life would become tolerable there only by the spirit growing into harmony with the scene, wild and solemn as the objects around it.

After her return to England in 1836, Miss Martineau continued to write on abolition, religion, and on the changes needed in society to give employment to women.

Harriet Martineau, Society in America. *London: Saunders and Otley, 1837; reprinted, New York: AMS Press, 1966. Vol. I, ix–x, xvi, xvii–xviii; III, 147–48, 150–51. And her* Retrospect of Western Travel. *London: Saunders and Otley, and New York: Harper, 1838. Vol. I, 139, 140–41, 142; II, 23, 54, 121–22, 164.*

7

Fanny Kemble and Slavery

Frances Anne Kemble (1809–1893), a young English actress traveling with her famous actor father, Charles Kemble, regarded her trip to the United States as a form of exile. Much of her journal during the two years after her arrival in 1832 detailed their stage performances, which were highly popular. In 1834 Fanny met Pierce Butler, a charming young Philadelphian. Not until after they were married did she discover that his wealth came from cotton and rice plantations in Georgia. Two daughters were born, in 1835 and 1838, and when the youngest was a baby the family went to Butler's plantations on islands near Darien, Georgia. There she wrote long letters addressed (though not sent) to her friend Elizabeth Sedgwick, of Lenox, Massachusetts. At first she was quite pleased with all things American, except for slavery.

1832

In beholding this fine young giant of a world, with all its magnificent capabilities for greatness, I think every Englishman must feel unmingled regret at the unjust and unwise course of policy which alienated such a child from the parent government. . . . No one, beholding this enormous country, stretching from ocean to ocean, watered with ten thousand glorious rivers, combining every variety of climate and soil, therefore, every variety of produce and population; possessing within itself every resource that other nations are forced either to buy abroad, or to create substitutes for at home; no one, seeing the internal wealth of America, the abundant fertility of the earth's surface, the riches heaped below it, the unparalleled facilities

46

for the intercourse of men, and the interchange of their possessions throughout its vast extent, can for an instant indulge the thought that such a country was ever destined to be an appendage to any other in the world.

With regard to what I have said . . . of the many reasons which combined to render this country independent of all others, I think they in some measure tell against the probability of its long remaining at unity with itself. Such numerous and clashing interests; such strong and opposite individuality of character between the northern and southern states; above all, such enormous extent of country; seem rationally to present many points of insecurity; many probabilities of separations and breakings asunder; but all this lies far on, and I leave it to those who have good eyes for a distance.

This country is in one respect blessed above all others, and above all others deserving of blessing. There are no poor—I say there are none, there *need* be none; none here need lift up the despairing voice of hopeless and helpless want, towards that Heaven which hears when men will not. No father here need work away his body's health, and his spirit's strength, in unavailing labour, from day to day, and from year to year, bowed down by the cruel curse his fellows lay upon him. No mother need wish, in the bitterness of her heart, that the children of her breast had died before they exhausted that nourishment which was the only one her misery could feel assured would not fail them. None need be born to vice, for none are condemned to abject poverty. . . . Thrice blessed is this country, for no such crying evil exists in its bosom; no such moral reproach, no such political rottenness.

To teach a slave to read or write is to incur a penalty either of fine or imprisonment. They form the larger proportion of the population, by far; and so great is the dread of insurrection on the part of the white inhabitants, that they are kept in the most brutish ignorance, and too often treated with the most brutal barbarity, in order to insure their subjection. Oh! what a breaking asunder of old manacles there will be, some of these fine days; what a fearful rising of the black flood; what a sweeping away, as by a torrent, of oppressions and tyrannies; what a fierce and horrible retaliation and revenge for wrong so long endured—so wickedly inflicted.

In 1839 Fanny insisted that she and the children should accompany Butler (whom she does not name in her journal) to his Georgia plantation.

DARIEN, GEORGIA, 1839

Cut off as I am here from all the usual resources and amusements of civilized existence, I shall find but little to communicate to you that is not furnished by my observations on the novel appearance of external nature, and the moral and physical condition of Mr. [Butler]'s people. . . .*

Miss Martineau . . . was purposely misled by the persons to whom she addressed her inquiries, who did not scruple to disgrace themselves by imposing in the grossest manner upon her credulity and anxiety to obtain information. It is a knowledge of this very shameful proceeding which has made me most especially anxious to avoid *fact hunting*. I might fill my letters to you with accounts received from others, but as I am aware of the risk which I run in so doing, I shall furnish you with no details but those which come under my own immediate observation.

I walked down the settlement toward the Infirmary or hospital, calling in at one or two of the houses along the row. These cabins consist of one room, about twelve feet by fifteen, with a couple of closets smaller and closer than the staterooms of a ship, divided off from the main room and each other by rough wooden partitions, in which the inhabitants sleep. They have almost all of them a rude bedstead, with the gray moss of

*In the original printing, Fanny's blank spaces for names are represented by dashes.

the forests for mattress, and filthy, pestilential-looking blankets for covering. Two families (sometimes eight and ten in number) reside in one of these huts, which are mere wooden frames pinned, as it were, to the earth by a brick chimney outside, whose enormous aperture within pours down a flood of air, but little counteracted by the miserable spark of fire, which hardly sends an attenuated thread of lingering smoke up its huge throat. A wide ditch runs immediately at the back of these dwellings, which is filled and emptied daily by the tide. Attached to each hovel is a small scrap of ground for a garden, which, however, is for the most part untended and uncultivated.

Such of these dwellings as I visited today were filthy and wretched in the extreme, and exhibited that most deplorable consequence of ignorance and an abject condition, the inability of the inhabitants to secure and improve even such pitiful comfort as might yet be achieved by them. Instead of the order, neatness, and ingenuity which might convert even these miserable hovels into tolerable residences, there was the careless, reckless, filthy indolence which even the brutes do not exhibit in their lairs and nests, and which seemed incapable of applying to the uses of existence the few miserable means of comfort yet within their reach. Firewood and shavings lay littered about the floors, while the half-naked children were cowering round two or three smouldering cinders. The moss with which the chinks and crannies of their ill-protecting dwellings might have been stuffed was trailing in dirt and dust about the ground, while the back door of the huts, opening upon a most unsightly ditch, was left wide open for the fowls and ducks, which they are allowed to raise, to travel in and out, increasing the filth of the cabin by what they brought and left in every direction.

In the midst of the floor, or squatting round the cold hearth, would be four or five little children from four to ten years old, the latter all with babies in their arms, the care of the infants being taken from the mothers (who are driven afield as soon as they recover from child labor), and devolved upon these poor little nurses, as they are called, whose business it is to watch the infant, and carry it to its mother whenever it may require nourishment. To these hardly human little beings I addressed my remonstrances about the filth, cold, and unnecessary wretchedness of their room, bidding the older boys and girls kindle up the fire, sweep the floor, and expel the poultry.

For a long time my very words seemed unintelligible to them, till, when I began to sweep and make up the fire, etc., they first fell to laughing, and then imitating me. . . .

Thus I traveled down the "street," in every dwelling endeavoring to awaken a new perception, that of cleanliness, sighing, as I went, over the futility of my own exertions, for how can slaves be improved? Nathless, thought I, let what can be done; for it may be that, the two being incompatible, improvement may yet expel slavery; and so it might, and surely would, if, instead of beginning at the end, I could but begin at the beginning of my task. If the mind and soul were awakened, instead of mere physical good attempted, the physical good would result, and the great curse vanish away; but my hands are tied fast, and this corner of the work is all that I may do.

Yet it cannot be but, from my words and actions, some revelations should reach these poor people; and going in and out among them perpetually, I shall teach, and they learn involuntarily a thousand things of deepest import. They must learn, and who can tell the fruit of that knowledge alone, that there are beings in the world, even with skins of a different color from their own, who have sympathy for their misfortunes, love for their virtues, and respect for their common nature— but oh! my heart is full almost to bursting as I walk among these most poor creatures.

The Infirmary is a large two-story building, terminating the broad orange-planted space between the two rows of houses which form the first settlement; it is built of whitewashed wood, and contains four large-sized rooms. But how shall I describe to you the spectacle which was presented to me on entering the first of these? But half the casements, of which there were six, were glazed, and these were obscured with dirt, almost as much as the other windowless ones were darkened by the dingy shutters, which the shivering inmates had fastened to in order to protect themselves from the cold.

A romanticized sketch, made in the 1850s, of General Philip Schuyler with Frederica, Baroness von Riedesel (1746–1808), and her children after the surrender of General Burgoyne at Saratoga in 1777, when she became a prisoner of war. *Engraved for Benson J. Lossing,* Pictorial Field-Book of the Revolution, Vol. I. *(New York: Harper, 1855).*

Frances Milton Trollope (1780–1863), an English writer, spent several years (1827–1831) traveling in the United States. Her sweet and demure appearance in this portrait seems at odds with her acid comments on the manners and customs of Americans, which were much resented by her hosts. This portrait, by Auguste Hervieu, was used as a frontispiece for the 5th edition of her *Domestic Manners of the Americans.* (*London: Bentley, 1839*).

The settlement at Nashoba, Tennessee, founded by Fanny Wright, was visited by the Englishwoman Frances Trollope in the winter of 1827–28. Traveling with her was an artist, Auguste Hervieu, who sketched this doleful view of the village. It was used, with some 23 other Hervieu sketches, to illustrate Trollope's *Domestic Manners of the Americans.* (*London: Whittaker, Treacher, 1832*).

The Lowell Girls were the first American women employed in factories. In the 1830's they operated looms in one of the many mills of Lowell, Massachusetts. Respectable young women from farm families, they were carefully chaperoned at work and in their boarding houses. The English visitor, Harriet Martineau (1802–1876), approved of the libraries and lyceums provided for them. This design for a bank-note vignette is in the New York Public Library Prints Division. *(Courtesy Print Collection, Miriam and Ira D. Wallach Division of Art, Prints and Photographs: The New York Public Library Astor, Lenox and Tilden Foundations.)*

Harriet Martineau (1802–1876), English scholar and writer, was thirty-two when she visited the United States. Her portrait by George Richmond, now in the National Portrait Gallery, London, shows her at the age of forty-eight.

Frances ("Fanny") Anne Kemble (1809–1893), an English actress, arrived in America with her actor father in 1832. Two years later she married a Philadelphian, Pierce Butler, who owned cotton and rice plantations in Georgia. Conditions among the slaves there so horrified her that she eventually left Butler, but she spent many of her remaining years in the United States. The engraved portrait was made by J. G. Stodard from the original painting by Thomas Sully, formerly owned by Kemble's daughter Frances Leigh. Sully painted a number of portraits of Kemble, in various theatrical roles, which may account for the dreaminess of this one.

Frances ("Fanny") Wright, later D'Arusmont (1795–1852), a Scottish reformer and lecturer, first visited the United States in 1818. She returned in 1824 and spent much of her later life in America, where she was outspoken in behalf of women's rights. Her portrait was engraved by J. C. Buttre, as the frontispiece for Elizabeth Cady Stanton, Susan B. Anthony, and Matilda Joslyn Gage, *The History of Woman Suffrage*, Vol. I. *(New York: Fowler and Wells, 1881).*

Henrietta-Lucy Dillon, Countess (later Marquise) de La Tour du Pin (1770–1853), escaped with her husband and two children from France during the Reign of Terror in 1794; they spent three years farming in New York State. Her elaborate coiffure establishes her as a member of the French aristocracy rather than as an American farmer. The engraving was used as the frontispiece of her *Recollections of the Revolution and the Empire,* tr. Walter Geer. *(New York: Brentano's, 1920).*

In the enormous chimney glimmered the powerless embers of a few sticks of wood, round which, however, as many of the sick women as could approach were cowering, some on wooden settles, most of them on the ground, excluding those who were too ill to rise; and these last poor wretches lay prostrate on the floor, without bed, mattress, or pillow, buried in tattered and filthy blankets, which, huddled round them as they lay strewed about, left hardly space to move upon the floor.

And here, in their hour of sickness and suffering, lay those whose health and strength are spent in unrequited labor for us—those who, perhaps even yesterday, were being urged on to their unpaid task—those whose husbands, fathers, brothers, and sons were even at that hour sweating over the earth, whose produce was to buy for us all the luxuries which health can revel in, all the comforts which can alleviate sickness. I stood in the midst of them, perfectly unable to speak, the tears pouring from my eyes at this sad spectacle of their misery, myself and my emotion alike strange and incomprehensible to them.

Here lay women expecting every hour the terrors and agonies of child-birth, others who had just brought their doomed offspring into the world, others who were groaning over the anguish and bitter disappointment of miscarriages—here lay some burning with fever, others chilled with cold and aching with rheumatism, upon the hard cold ground, the draughts and dampness of the atmosphere increasing their sufferings, and dirt, noise, and stench, and every aggravation of which sickness is capable, combined in their condition—here they lay like brute beasts, absorbed in physical suffering; unvisited by any of those Divine influences which may ennoble the dispensations of pain and illness, forsaken, as it seemed to me, of all good; and yet, O God, Thou surely hadst not forsaken them!

Now pray take notice that this is the hospital of an estate where the owners are supposed to be humane, the overseer efficient and kind, and the negroes remarkably well cared for and comfortable.

As soon as I recovered from my dismay, I addressed old Rose the midwife, who had charge of this room, bidding her open the shutters of such windows as were glazed, and let in the light. I next proceeded to make up the fire; but, upon my lifting a log for that purpose, there was one universal outcry of horror, and old Rose, attempting to snatch it from me, exclaimed: "Let alone, missis—let be; what for you lift wood? you have nigger enough, missis, to do it!" I hereupon had to explain to them my view of the purposes for which hands and arms were appended to our bodies, and forthwith began making Rose tidy up the miserable apartment, removing all the filth and rubbish from the floor that could be removed, folding up in piles the blankets of the patients who were not using them, and placing, in rather more sheltered and comfortable positions, those who were unable to rise.

It was all that I could do, and having enforced upon them all my earnest desire that they should keep their room swept, and as tidy as possible, I passed on to the other room on the ground floor, and to the two above, one of which is appropriated to the use of the men who are ill. They were all in the same deplorable condition, the upper rooms being rather the more miserable, inasmuch as none of the windows were glazed at all, and they had, therefore, only the alternative of utter darkness, or killing draughts of air from the unsheltered casements. In all, filth, disorder, and misery abounded; the floor was the only bed, and scanty begrimed rags of blankets the only covering.

I left this refuge for Mr. [Butler]'s sick dependents with my clothes covered with dust, and full of vermin, and with a heart heavy enough, as you will well believe. My morning's work had fatigued me not a little, and I was glad to return to the house, where I gave vent to my indignation and regret at the scene I had just witnessed to Mr. [Butler] and his overseer, who, here, is a member of our family. The latter told me that the condition of the hospital had appeared to him, from his first entering upon his situation (only within the last year), to require a reform, and that he had proposed it to the former manager, Mr. K[ing], and Mr. [Butler]'s brother, who is part proprietor of the estate, but, receiving no encouragement from them, had supposed that it was a matter of indifference to the owners, and had left it in the condition in which he had found it, in which condition it has been for the last nineteen years and upward. . . .

I forgot to tell you that in the hospital were several sick babies, whose mothers were permitted to suspend their field labor in order to nurse them. Upon addressing some remonstrances to one of these, who, besides having a sick child, was ill herself, about the horribly dirty condition of her baby, she assured me that it was impossible for them to keep their children clean; that they went out to work at daybreak, and did not get their tasks done till evening, and that then they were too tired and worn out to do any thing but throw themselves down and sleep. This statement of hers I mentioned on my return from the hospital, and the overseer appeared extremely annoyed by it, and assured me repeatedly that it was not true.

How much I wished that, instead of music, and dancing, and such stuff, I had learned something of sickness and health, of the conditions and liabilities of the human body.

I have proclaimed to all the little baby nurses that I will give a cent to every little boy or girl whose baby's face shall be clean, and one to every individual with clean face and hands of their own. My appeal was fully comprehended by the majority, it seems, for this morning I was surrounded as soon as I came out, by a swarm of children carrying their little charges on their backs and in their arms, the shining, and, in many instances, wet faces and hands of the latter bearing ample testimony to the ablutions which had been inflicted upon them. How they will curse me and the copper cause of all their woes in their baby bosoms!

Do you know that, little as grown negroes are admirable for their personal beauty (in my opinion, at least), the black babies of a year or two old are very pretty; they have, for the most part, beautiful eyes and eyelashes, the pearly perfect teeth, which they retain after their other juvenile graces have left them; their skins are all (I mean of blacks generally) infinitely finer and softer than the skins of white people. . . .

I have seen many babies on this plantation who were quite as pretty as white children, and this very day stooped to kiss a little sleeping creature that lay on its mother's knees in the infirmary—as beautiful a specimen of a sleeping infant as I ever saw. The caress excited irrepressible delight of all the women present—poor creatures! who seemed to forget that I was a woman, and had children myself, and bore a woman's and a mother's heart toward them and theirs . . . had the question been my election, I am very sure nobody else would have had a chance of a vote through the island.

Today I have the pleasure of announcing to you a variety of improvements about to be made in the infirmary of the island. There is to be a third story—a mere loft, indeed—added to the building; but, by affording more room for the least distressing cases of sickness to be drafted off into, it will leave the ground floor and room above it comparatively free for the most miserable of these unfortunates. To my unspeakable satisfaction, these destitute apartments are to be furnished with bedsteads, mattresses, pillows, and blankets; and I feel a little comforted for the many heartaches my life here inflicts upon me—at least some of my twinges will have wrought this poor alleviation of their wretchedness for the slaves when prostrated by disease or pain.

I hope this sojourn among Mr. [Butler]'s slaves may not lessen my respect for him, but I fear it; for the details of slaveholding are so unmanly, letting alone every other consideration, that I know not how any one with the spirit of a man can condescend to them. . . . Mr. [Butler], of course, sees and feels none of this as I do, and, I should think, must regret that he ever brought me here, to have my abhorrence of the theory of slavery deepened, and strengthened every hour of my life, by what I see of its practice.

The sufferings of those who come to me for redress, and, still more, the injustice done to the great majority who can not, have filled my heart with bitterness and indignation that have overflowed my lips, till, I suppose, [Mr. Butler] is weary of hearing what he has never heard before, the voice of passionate expostulation and importunate pleading against wrongs that he will not even acknowledge, and for creatures whose common humanity with his own I half think he does not believe; but I must return to the North, for my condition would be almost worse than theirs—condemned to hear and see so much wretchedness, not only without the means of alleviating it, but without permission even to represent it for alleviation; this is no place for me, since I was not born among slaves, and cannot bear to live among them.

I cannot give way to the bitter impatience I feel at my present position, and come back to the North without leaving my babies; . . . I must, for their sakes, remain where they are, and learn this dreary lesson of human suffering to the end.

Fanny's last letter from the plantation was written in April 1839. When she left the South, she took with her the hastily-written journal. Fanny amended it and made a fair copy which had a limited circulation among her friends and which she considered publishing. However, she was still attached to Butler and felt publication would be unfair to him.

During the next ten years Fanny was torn between her affection for Butler, as well as her duty to him and the children, and her sense of moral outrage at the tainted source of their livelihood. In 1849 Butler sued for divorce, which was granted, with custody of the daughters given to their father.

The Journal *was eventually published in 1863, the year the slaves were emancipated. It was too late for its shocking revelations to change the course of history.*

Fanny returned to the stage and for some twenty years she gave public readings from Shakespeare, in both America and England.

Frances Anne Kemble (later Butler), The Journal of Frances Anne Butler. *London: John Murray, 1835; reprinted, New York: Benjamin Blom, 1970. Vol. I, 237–39, 213–14 note; II, 36–37. And her* Journal of a Residence on a Georgian Plantation in 1838–1839. *New York: Harper, 1863. Pages 16–17, 30–36, 38, 40–41, 79–80, 115–16, 122, 170–71, 174.*

8

Anna Jameson on the Chippewa Indians

Anna Brownell Murphy Jameson (1794–1860) was an Irish archae-ologist, a well-known writer and art critic. She came to Canada in the winter of 1838. Her husband, Robert Jameson, from whom she sepa-rated shortly after their marriage in 1825, was running for an office in Canada and she wished to support his bid. She spent a bleak winter in Ontario and in early June she traveled to Mackinac and Sault Ste Marie. She was much interested in the Indians and had fallen into the best company to give her entrée to the Great Lakes Tribes. She traveled with two daughters of the then-deceased Irish trader John Johnston, from Sault Ste Marie. Johnston's widow, Charlotte (Anna called her Neengai), was the full-blood daughter of a Chippewa chief, and one of her daughters was married to a pioneer authority on the Great Lakes Tribes, an Indian agent at Mackinac.

AT THE FALLS OF ST. MARY'S, JULY 1838

The more I looked upon these glancing, dancing rapids, the more resolute I grew to venture myself in the midst of them. George Johnston [perhaps related to Charlotte Johnston] went to seek a fit canoe and a dextrous steersman. . . .

The canoe being ready, I went up to the top of the portage and we launched into the river. It was a small fishing canoe about ten feet long, quite new, and light and elegant and buoyant as a bird on the waters. I reclined on a mat at the

56

bottom, Indian fashion (there are no seats in a genuine Indian canoe); in a minute we were within the verge of the rapids, and down we went, with a whirl and a splash!—the white surge leaping around me—over me. The Indian with astonishing dexterity kept the head of the canoe to the breakers, and somehow or other we danced through them. I could see, as I looked over the edge of the canoe, that the passage between the rocks was sometimes not more than two feet in width, and we had to turn sharp angles—a touch of which would have sent us to destruction—all this I could see through the transparent eddying waters, but I can truly say, I had not even a momentary sensation of fear, but rather of giddy, breathless, delicious excitement. I could even admire the beautiful attitude of a fisher, past whom we swept as we came to the bottom. The whole affair, from the moment I entered the canoe till I reached the landing place, occupied seven minutes, and the distance is about three quarters of a mile.

My Indians were enchanted, and when I reached *home*, my good friends were not less delighted at my exploit: they told me I was the first European female who had ever performed it, and assuredly I shall not be the last. I recommend it as an exercise before breakfast. As for my Neengai, she laughed, clapped her hands, and embraced me several times. I was declared duly initiated, and adopted into the family by the name of Wah,sàh,ge,wah,nó,quà. They had already called me among themselves, in reference to my complexion and my travelling propensities, O,daw,yaun,gee, *the fair changing moon*, or rather, *the fair moon which changes her place:* but now, in compliment to my successful achievement, Mrs. Johnston bestowed this new appellation, which I much prefer. It signifies *the bright foam*, or more properly, with the feminine adjunct, *qua, the woman of the bright foam*; and by this name I am henceforth to be known among the Chippewas.

A large tract of Sugar Island is [Neengai's] property; and this year she manufactured herself three thousand five hundred weight of sugar of excellent quality. In the fall, she goes up with her people in canoes to the entrance of Lake Superior, to fish in the bays and creeks for a fortnight, and comes back with a load of fish cured for the winter's consumption. In her youth she hunted, and was accounted the surest eye and fleetest foot among the women of her tribe. Her talents, energy, activity, and strength of mind, and her skill in all the domestic avocations of the Indian women, have maintained comfort and plenty within her dwelling in spite of the losses sustained by her husband [after the War of 1812], while her descent from the blood of their ancient chiefs renders her an object of great veneration among the Indians around, who, in all their miseries, maladies, and difficulties, apply to her for aid or for counsel.

There is one subject on which all travellers in these regions— all who have treated of the manners and modes of life of the north-west tribes, are accustomed to expatiate with great eloquence and indignation, which they think it incumbent on the gallantry and chivalry of Christendom to denounce, as constituting the true badge and distinction of barbarism and heathenism, opposed to civilisation and Christianity:—I mean the treatment and condition of their women. The women, they say, are "drudges," "slaves," "beasts of burthen," victims, martyrs, degraded, abject, oppressed; that not only the cares of the household and maternity, but the cares and labours proper to the men, fall upon them; and they seem to consider no expression of disapprobation, and even abhorrence, too strong for the occasion; and if there be any who should feel inclined to modify such objurgations, or speak in excuse or mitigation of the fact, he might well fear that the publication of such opinions would expose him, in every review, to the death of Orpheus or Pentheus.

Luckily I have no such risk to run. Let but my woman's wit bestead me here as much as my womanhood, and I will, as the Indians say,"tell you a piece of my mind," and place the matter before you in another point of view.

Under one aspect of the question, all these gentlemen travellers are right; they are right in their estimate of the condition of the Indian squaws—they *are* drudges, slaves: and they are right in the opinion, that the condition of the women in any community is a test of the advance of moral and intellectual cultivation in that community; . . .

Take into consideration, in the first place, that in these Indian communities the task of providing subsistence falls solely and entirely on the men. When it is said, in general terms, that the men do nothing but *hunt* all day, while the women are engaged in perpetual *toil*, I suppose this suggests to civilised readers the idea of a party of gentlemen at Melton, or a turnout of Mr. Meynell's hounds; or at most a deer-stalking excursion to the Highlands—a holiday affair; while the women, poor souls! must sit at home and sew, and spin, and cook victuals. But what is really the life of an Indian hunter?—one of incessant, almost killing toil, and often danger. A hunter goes out at dawn, knowing that, if he returns empty, his wife and his little ones must *starve*—no uncommon predicament! . . .

Where, then, the whole duty and labour of providing the means of subsistence, ennobled by danger and courage, fall upon the man, the woman naturally sinks in importance, and is a dependent drudge. But she is not therefore, I suppose, so *very* miserable, nor, relatively, so very abject; she is sure of protection; sure of maintenance, at least while the man has it; sure of kind treatment; sure that she will never have her children taken from her but by death; sees none better off than herself, and has no conception of a superior destiny; and it is evident that in such a state the appointed and necessary share of the woman is the household work, and all other domestic labour. . . .

Hence, however hard the lot of the woman, she is in no *false* position. The two sexes are in their natural and true position relatively to the state of society, and the means of subsistence. . . .

Lewis and Clarke, in exploring the Missouri, came upon a tribe of Indians who, from local circumstances, kill little game, and live principally on fish and roots; and as the women are equally expert with the men in procuring subsistence, they have a rank and influence very rarely found among Indians. The females are permitted to speak freely before the men, to whom indeed they sometimes address themselves in a tone of authority. On many subjects their judgment and opinion are respected, and in matters of trade their advice is generally asked and pursued; the labours of the family too are shared equally.

Attempts of a noble and a fated race, to oppose, or even to delay for a time, the rolling westward of the great tide of civilisation, are like efforts to dam up the rapids of Niagara. The moral world has its laws, fixed as those of physical nature. The hunter must make way before the agriculturist, and the Indian must learn to take the bit between his teeth, and set his hand to the ploughshare, or *perish*. As yet I am inclined to think that the idea of the Indians becoming what *we* call a civilised people seems quite hopeless; those who entertain such benevolent anticipations should come here, and behold the effect which three centuries of contact with the whites have produced on the nature and habits of the Indian. The benevolent theorists in England should come and see with their own eyes that there is a bar to the civilisation of the Indians, and the increase or even preservation of their numbers, which no power can overleap. Their own principle, that "the Great Spirit did indeed create both the red man and the white man, but created them essentially different in nature and manners," is not, perhaps, far from the truth.

Take, for instance, the following scene, as described with great naïveté by one of the Moravian missionaries. After a conference with some of the Delaware chief men, in which they were informed that these missionaries had come to teach them a better and purer religion, of which the one fundamental principle, leading to eternal salvation, was belief in the Redeemer, and atonement through his blood for the sins of all mankind—all of which was contained in the book which he held in his hand,—"Wangoman, a great chief and medicine man among them, rose to reply. He began by tracing two lines on the ground, and endeavoured to explain that there were two ways which led alike to God and to happiness, the way of the Red man, and the way of the White man, but the way of the

Red man, he said, was the straighter and the shorter of the two."

The missionary here interposed, and represented that God himself had descended on earth to teach men the *true* way. Wangoman declared that "he had been intimately acquainted with God for many years, and had never heard that God became a man and shed his blood, and therefore the God of whom Brother Zeisberger preached could not be the true God, or he, Wangoman, would have been made acquainted with the circumstance." . . .

What should the red man see in the civilisation of the white man which should move him to envy or emulation, or raise in his mind a wish to exchange his "own unshackled life, and his innate capacities of soul," for our artificial social habits, our morals, which are contradicted by our opinions, and our religion, which is violated both in our laws and our lives?

Here it is the selfishness of the white man which speaks; that it is for his interest, and for his worldly advantage, that the red man should be removed out of his way, and be thrust back from the extending limits of civilisation—even like these forests, which fall before us, and vanish from the earth, leaving for a while some decaying stumps and roots over which the plough goes in time, and no vestige remains to say that here they *have been*. . . . Wherever the Christian comes, he brings the Bible in one hand, disease, corruption, and the accursed fire-water, in the other; or flinging down the book of peace, he boldly and openly proclaims that might gives right, and substitutes the sabre and the rifle for the slower desolation of starvation and whisky.

Mrs. Jameson's two months of travel into the north woods ended when she returned from the Manitoulin Islands with the Indian superintendent. She was the only woman in a party of twenty-two. They traveled by birch-bark canoe, slept out of doors, and cooked over campfires. The journey ended in Penetanguishene, on Georgian Bay.

There was an inn here, not the worst of Canadian inns; and the *wee* closet called a bed-room, and the little bed with its white cotton curtains appeared to me the *ne plus ultra* of luxury. I recollect walking in and out of the room ten times a day for the mere pleasure of contemplating it, and anticipated with impatience the moment when I should throw myself down into it, and sleep once more on a christian bed. But nine nights passed in the open air, or on rocks, and on boards, had spoiled for me the comforts of civilisation, and to sleep *on a bed* was impossible; I was smothered, I was suffocated, and altogether wretched and fevered;—I sighed for my rock on Lake Huron.

Anna spent the rest of her life in London, with excursions to Italy and Germany. She had a wide circle of literary friends, including Lady Byron and Elizabeth Barrett Browning. She accompanied Elizabeth and Robert Browning to Italy after their marriage.

Anna Jameson, Sketches in Canada and Rambles Among the Red Men. *London: Longman, 1852. Pages 241-42, 249–50, 288–91, 125–28, 307. This work reprinted part of her* Winter Studies and Summer Rambles in Canada, *published in 1838.*

9

Fredrika Bremer's Impressions of Women

Fredrika Bremer (1801–1865) was a famous Swedish novelist and traveler. She had chosen to remain single and to dedicate herself to aiding the distressed and to speaking for women through the medium of the domestic novel. She had read the works of earlier travelers to the United States but wished to see the new democracy for herself. She arrived in October 1849 and remained until September 1851, traveling constantly and writing thousands of pages of letters to family and friends.

BROOKLYN, NOVEMBER 5, 1849

The effect of my American journey, as far as myself am concerned, is altogether quite different to what I expected. I came hither to breathe a new and fresher atmosphere of life; to observe the popular life, institutions, and circumstances of a new country; to become clearer in my own mind on certain questions connected with the development of nations and people; and, in particular, to study the women and the homes of the New World, and from the threshold of the home to obtain a view of the future of humanity, because, as the river is born from the springs of heaven, so is the life and the fate of a people born from the hidden life of the home.

I came, in a word, to occupy myself with public affairs; and it is private affairs, it is the individual which seizes upon my interest, my feelings, my thoughts. I came with a secret intention of breaking myself loose from fiction and its subjects, and of living with thinkers for other purposes; and I am compelled toward it more forcibly than ever; compelled involuntarily, both by thought and feeling, toward fiction; compelled to bring into life forms, scenes, and circumstances, which, as dim shadows, have for twenty years existed in the background of my soul. And in this so-called realist country, but which has more poetical life in it than people have any idea of in Europe, have I already *in petto*, experienced and written more of the romance of life than I have done for many years.

PHILADELPHIA, JULY 15

Ah, my child, how delighted I am with the drawing academy for young girls which I visited yesterday! It is an excellent institution, and will effect an infinite deal of good. Here genius and the impulse for cultivation in young women may receive nourishment and development, and patient industry and the power of labor have occupation and pecuniary profit in the most agreeable way.

Young girls can receive instruction at this academy (the poor free of cost, the more wealthy on the payment of a small sum) in drawing, painting, composition; in the making of designs for woven fabrics, carpets, or paper-hangings; in wood engraving, lithography, &c.; and the establishment has already been so successful, and so great is the progress made by the pupils, so numerous are the orders for designs, wood engraving, &c., and so well paid is all, that the young girls are able already to make considerable earnings, and there is every prospect that the establishment will, within very few years, be able fully to support itself.

It is the same school which I saw last year in its infancy, with the warm-hearted Mrs. [Sarah] P[eter], the wife of the British consul here, when it entirely depended on her support. Since then it has rapidly developed itself, has become incorporated with the excellent Franklin Institute here, and receives an annual stipend from its funds, and now grows from its own strength. Several of the young pupils gain already from ten to fifteen dollars per week. The publisher of "Sartain's Magazine" told me that the demand for such work in the United States, for newspapers, magazines, manufactures, &c., was so great, that all the women of the country, who had time to devote themselves to such occupation, might have full employment. And never have I seen, in any school whatever, so many cheerful, animated countenances. . . .

I am very much pleased with this academy also, because its design is applicable to Sweden; and may there open a prospect for many a one in the improvement of both soul and body. I have brought away with me many proofs and specimens, which have been kindly given to me, as well as all the information which I could obtain.

Ah! let us, if possible, establish almshouses and asylums for the old, the infirm, and the sick; but for the young, let us give *work*—free scope for emulation; let us unfold paths for their development, and noble objects for their lives.

The same excellent and agreeable gentleman (Dr. E.) who took me to the drawing academy, accompanied me to-day to the medical college for ladies, which was established here a year ago, and which will enable ladies to receive a scientific education as physicians. This institution has not been established without great opposition, but it has nevertheless come into operation, to the honor of the spirit and justice of the New World!

To this ought also to be added the steadfastness and talent of a young American woman, and the reputation which she obtained abroad. Elizabeth Blackwell, after having for several years, by hard work, helped to educate and maintain several younger sisters, devoted herself to the profession of medicine, firmly resolved to open in this way a career for herself and other women. She was met by a thousand difficulties; prejudice and ill will threw impediments in every step; but she overcame all; and finally studied and graduated as physician at the city of Geneva, in Western New York. After this she went abroad, desirous of entering and passing the Medical College of Paris.

The head of the college was shocked: "You must dress yourself as a man," said he, "otherwise it will be quite impossible."

"I shall not alter even a ribbon on my bonnet!" said she; "do as you will; but your conduct shall be made known. You have seen my certificate; you have no right to refuse me admission."

Mr. L. was obliged to comply. Elizabeth's womanly dignity and bearing, added to her remarkable knowledge, impressed the professors as well as students of the college. . . . Dr. E. wished me to become acquainted with this young woman—this vigorous soul in a slender and delicate frame—whom he cordially admires, and rejoices over as with paternal pride. He said, speaking of her to me.

"She is not taller than you, but she would take you under one arm and my daughter under the other, and run up stairs with you both."

I should like to see that. . . .

It seems to me very desirable that this establishment should direct the attention of the female students, or rather that they should themselves direct it, to that portion of medical science which pre-eminently belongs to them; for is there not here, as in all spheres of life, science, arts, and professions, one region which, beyond all others, belongs to woman, by reason of natural tendencies? In medicine, it is evidently partly the *preventive*—that is to say, by attention to health and diet, to effect the prevention of disease, especially in women and children— and partly, *par excellence, healing, curing.* Women have in all ages shown a remarkable talent for the healing art—have shown an ability, by herbs and the so-called domestic medicine, to cure or assuage human suffering. Their branch of medical art ought evidently to be that of the alleviation of pain; they should not be the instigators of suffering. In this they would make great progress. The instincts of the heart would be united in them with the knowledge of the head. Curative medicine would therefore be more adapted to them than surgery. . . .

Oh, to be young, to be able to devote a life to this glorious science!

NAHANT, MASSACHUSETTS, AUGUST 1, 1851

I had in the evening the great pleasure of conversing with two cultivated and thinking women of my acquaintance about the ladies of America—of that deficiency of many-sided development, that deficiency of instinct for the higher human interests, and of that want of the ability for conversation which is found in so great a number.

These amiable ladies, themselves distinguished in all respects agree with me in many of my observations, and, like myself, can not see any means of alleviating these deficiencies, excepting by a more thorough system of cultivation, a more broad and general development of mind; and many are the signs which will make this inevitable, if women will maintain the esteem of their own sex as well as that of the men. Men have in general, at this time, more gallantry than actual esteem for women. They are polite to them, ready to comply with their wishes; but they regard them evidently more as pretty children than as their reasonable equals, and do not give them their society when they seek strengthening food for soul and thought. The many beautiful examples which one meets of an opposite, of a perfect relationship between the two sexes, can not be said to belong to the rule. Women are, it is true, rulers in the home and in social life, but that is frequently rather through their weaknesses than their virtues.

We spake of the signs which are indicative of the approach of a better state of things. We saw it by degrees gradually advancing in the public consciousness, and we marked also, as the forerunner of this, the Rights of Woman Conventions, which have now been held annually for some years in the Northern States. The holding of these Conventions is a movement of transition, which will cease of itself when the end is attained. Many true and profound thoughts were expressed in the last great Convention which was held last year in Massachusetts, and at which thousands of both men and women were present; excellent speeches were delivered, beautiful speeches, worthy of those distinguished speakers.

Among these thoughts I in particular remember what was said on the life and culture of past ages in comparison with those of the present time.

Occupations and objects in life do not now separate the sexes, as was the case formerly. Man, except only in occasional instances, does not now live for the warlike profession; he does not now practice, above every thing else, strength of body and achievements of arms; the two sexes have, in a more spiritual sphere of life, come nearer to each other in the home and social life. Woman becomes more and more the companion and helpmate of man; his powers of soul will be crippled or elevated in proportion as he finds in her that which retards or animates them. And the circumscribing of her development will operate unfavorably upon himself.

This was said, but far better than I have said it, by Mrs. Paulina Davis, the lovely president of the Convention, that pale lady with the noble features and expression of countenance, and the rich golden hair, whom I saw at my good female doctor's, Miss H[arriot Hunt].

NEW YORK, SEPTEMBER 4, 1851

While I am on the subject of woman's position in society, and Women's Rights' Conventions, I will say a few words about them. I am very glad of the latter, because they cause many facts, and many good thoughts to become public. I rejoice at the nobility and prudence with which many female speakers stand forth; at the profound truths, worthy of all consideration, which many of them utter; at the depth of woman's experience of life, her sufferings, and yearnings, which through them come to light; I rejoice and am amazed to see so many distinguished men sympathize in this movement, and support the women in their public appearance, often presenting the subject in language still stronger than they themselves use. I rejoice also that society, with decision peculiar to the Anglo-American spirit of association, has so rapidly advanced from talking to action—has divided into separate committees, for the development of the separate branches of the subject, preparatory to new social arrangements.

But I do not rejoice at some lesser, well-intentioned measures and steps which have been proposed; do not rejoice at the tone of accusation and bravado which has now and then been assumed in the Convention, and at several expressions less noble and beautiful. . . .

Conventions are good, because they give emphasis to the great new moment of life in the community; they are good as a sifting wind separating the chaff from the wheat. They will, if rightly conducted, hasten on the approaching day; if otherwise, they will retard it.

THE PHALANSTERY, NEW JERSEY, 1851

Many of the young ladies made their appearance at the ball in the so-called Bloomer costume, that is to say, short dresses made to the throat, and trowsers. This costume, which is, in reality, much more modest than that of the ordinary ball-room, and which looks extremely well on young ladies in their every-day occupations, is not advantageous for a ball-room, and is not at all becoming in the waltz, unless the skirts are very short, which was the case with two otherwise remarkably well-dressed and very pretty young girls. Some of them had really in their Bloomer costume a certain fantastic grace; but when I compared this with the true feminine grace which exhibited itself in some young girls with long dresses, and in other respects equally modest attire with the Bloomer ladies, I could not but give the palm to the long dresses.

Fredrika Bremer, The Homes of the New World: Impressions of America, *tr. by Mary Howitt. New York: Harper, 1858. Vol. I, 53–54; II, 553–57, 568–70, 615, 618.*

10

Theresa Pulszky Visits Lucretia Mott and Dines at the White House

Theresa Pulszky (b. 1815) and her husband, Francis Pulszky, were untitled members of the Hungarian nobility. They were supporters of the revolutionary leader, Louis Kossuth, and in 1849, after the collapse of freed Hungary, all three were forced to flee their country. When Congress rescued Kossuth from exile in Turkey and invited him to visit the United States, the Pulszkys accompanied him. They arrived in December 1851 and spent six months touring the country, honoring Kossuth and raising funds for the liberation of Hungary.

PHILADELPHIA, DECEMBER 25, 1851

I called on Mrs. Mott, the eminent Quaker lady, to whom a mutual friend had given me a letter.

I have seldom seen a face more artistically beautiful than that of Mrs. Lucretia Mott. She looks like an antique cameo. Her features are so markedly characteristic, that, if they were less noble, they might be called sharp. Beholding her I felt that great ideas and noble purposes must have grown up with her mind, which have a singular power of expression in her very movements. Her language is, like her appearance, peculiar and transparent, and it is only when she touches upon the slavery question that her eye flashes with an indignation and her lips quiver with a hasty impatience, disturbing the placid harmony of her countenance and her conversation.

But though she so positively pronounces the views at which she has arrived by self-made inquiry, yet she mildly listens to every objection, and tries to convince by the power of her arguments, untinged by the slightest fanaticism. She expressed her warm sympathy with the cause of Hungary, and her admiration of the genius of Kossuth; yet she blamed his neutrality in the slavery question.

I objected, that as Kossuth claimed non-intervention as the sacred law of nations, he was not called to interfere in a domestic question of the United States, so intimately connected with her constitution. But how can Kossuth, the champion of liberty,—answered she—not raise his voice in favour of the oppressed race? to argue is surely not the same thing as to interfere.

I replied, that a question involving intricate domestic interests, and for that very reason passions so bitter, that even an allusion to it rouses sensitive jealousies, certainly cannot be discussed by a foreigner with the slightest chance of doing good; that the difficulty of emancipation lies perhaps less in the lack of acknowledgment of the evils of slavery, than in the hardness to advise the many of carrying emancipation without convulsing the financial interests of the slaveholders, and to do it in a constitutional way. For after all, this must be attended to, if the welfare of the whole community is not to be endangered, therefore this problem can only be solved practically by native American statesmen, living in the midst of the people, with whom is lodged the final power to adopt the measure, as it has already been done in the Free States and in the old Spanish colonies.

Though I could not acquiesce in the opinion of Mrs. Mott, that the abolition of slavery should be preached in season and out of season, by the defender of the rights of nations, I yet fell beneath the charm of her moral superiority, and I warmly wished that I could spend hours, to listen and to discuss with her and Mr. Mott, in the attractive circle of her children and grandchildren.

71

Great was, therefore, my astonishment, when, upon my expressing my admiration for Mrs. Mott to some gentlemen, one of them exclaimed, "You do not mean to say, that you have called on that lady?"

"Of course I have, was my answer; why should I not?—I am most gratified to have done so, and I only regret that the shortness of the time we have to spend here, prevents me from often repeating my visit."

"But she is a furious Abolitionist," retorted the gentleman.—"It will do great harm to Governor Kossuth, if you associate with that party."

"I perceive, sir,"—said I—"that you highly estimate Mrs. Mott, as you consider her alone a whole party. But if any friend of Governor Kossuth, even if he himself converses with a person who has strong opinions against slavery, what harm can there be in that?"

"Your cause will then lose many friends in this city," was the answer.

I was perfectly amazed at such intolerance, and expressed this frankly. The gentleman, however, attempted to point out to me what mischief the Abolitionists were doing, and how long ago emancipation would have been carried in all the States, had the Abolitionists not so violently interfered; and besides (continued he) Mrs. Mott preaches!

"Well," replied I, "do not many Quaker ladies preach occasionally?"

This fact was admitted, but another gentleman remarked, that Mrs. Mott was dangerous, as her sermons were powerfully inciting.

"Is she perhaps a fighting Quaker," enquired I, "who appeals to the words of the Saviour, that he did not come to send peace on earth, but the sword?"

"I am a fighting Quaker myself," said the gentleman, "my forefathers fought in the revolutionary war, but Mrs. Mott is a Hicksite."

To my enquiry, what were the tenets of the Hicksites inspiring such dislike, I got the answer, "They are very bad, very bad; they, in fact, believe nothing."

This assertion was so contradictory to the impression left on my mind by Mrs. Mott, that I attentively perused some of her sermons, and I found them pervaded by that fervent desire to seek truth and to do right, of which Jesus teaches us that blessed are they which do hunger and thirst after righteousness, for they shall be filled—and therefore, although my views differ from hers on many points, I perceived that party-feeling must be strong in Philadelphia, to arouse such unjust views as I had heard expressed, and I could not help thinking that the meddling and narrow spirit had not yet departed here, which, in 1707, proposed that young men should be obliged to marry at a certain age, and that only two sorts of clothes should be worn, one kind for summer, and one for winter.

As I later learnt, the Hicksites got their name from Elias Hicks, a celebrated preacher of the Society of Friends, who taught doctrines of Unitarian character, and got a considerable influence amongst the Quakers, which led to a disruption of this peaceful community. About three hundred congregations called themselves orthodox, and gave up communion with the other two hundred congregations, whom they since designate as Hicksites.

On the 6th of January we dined at the White House, the official abode of the President. Every one who is familiar with European "etiquette," and its traditional influence, must wonder how utterly every vestige of this kind has disappeared across the ocean. It is true that in Europe too, Spain perhaps excepted, etiquette has, since the first French Revolution, ceased to be what it is still in the East, *a code of the formalities of reverence*, whose laws are strictly enforced by education, and are religiously observed by habit. . . .

At the White House there is nothing of the kind to be seen. There are here no pictures, no statues, no silk tapestry, no costly furniture, scarcely a few prints, and even these are presents of the French artist who engraved them.

The appearance of the guests of the President is as simple as his abode. This formed one of the topics of my conversation with the President [Millard Fillmore], whose neighbour I was at table. He remarked that the people of the United States claimed economy in every detail from their chief magistrate, and that on one occasion, when an ex-President stood up for the Presidency, his opponents used the argument against him that he had introduced gilded spoons and elegant plate at the White House. Here it is only the intrinsic dignity of the personal character which can invest the President with social authority.

We read of Washington, "that he received visitors with a dignified bow, in a manner avoiding to shake hands, even with his best friends." But it certainly required the acknowledged superiority of "the father of the nation," that public opinion did not protest against such reserve; for to meet every one on terms of perfect equality, is the right and the custom of every American citizen.

Mr. Fillmore has, in his countenance and in his manners, an expression of natural kind-hearted frankness, fully in harmony with that principle: and Mrs. Fillmore resembles him in that respect. Their daughter has likewise imbibed this republican characteristic, and she unites with it an amiable sincerity, which struck me, when I remarked to her how very well she spoke French; on which she answered to me, that she had had opportunity to practise it in the school where she lately had been a teacher.

Such views, fostered and maintained by public opinion,—the absence of all military pageantry in the dress and household of the President, though he is the commander-in-chief of the army, navy, and militia,—is an insurmountable barrier against any thought of usurpation, and even the hand-shaking with everybody,—the most tiresome of all the Presidential duties,— has become one of the great guarantees of the republican institutions. It retains the chief magistrate on the level of the citizen, reminding him incessantly that he is but one of them.

And therefore it is not so painful for a President to return to private life as we should imagine. On the 3d of March, four years after his election, he removes quietly to a hotel in Washington, and having settled his domestic affairs, he again takes up his former profession. Jefferson goes to his plantation; John Quincy Adams recommences his political career, as member of the house of representatives; Tyler accepts a small municipal office in Virginia; and Mr. Fillmore will probably return to the office, where his junior partner has, during the time of his Presidency, conducted his law business.

A party of Indians, from the Far West, had arrived in Washington, with complaints and petitions to their "great father."

The President invited us to witness the audience in the White House. The chiefs and braves of four different tribes were here, and two of them had brought their squaws along with them; clad in their skins and blankets, or ornamented with feather crowns, with their clubs and pipes, crouching on the floor, they offered a most picturesque scene. They were really red, that is to say, they were *painted*; but, when washed, the red man is by no means red, but light-brown.

Mr. Fillmore, sitting in an arm-chair, surrounded by some of the government officials and the Indian agents, addressed his red children in the usual way, summoning them to explain the object of their visit. He did it with a dignity which struck me as different from his usual demeanour. The communications were made through several native interpreters, as the Indians did not all speak the same language.

The chiefs rose one after the other, shook hands with their "great father," and complained that the emigrants to California were incessantly crossing their hunting-grounds with horses and waggons, frightening away the deer, without giving compensation for the damage; that they had but small stores of Indian corn; that they feared starvation, and requested redress of their "great father."

One of the chiefs, an Otoe, mentioned that their tribe never had raised the tomahawk against their white brethren, and yet they were perishing, like the others. Another chief found that Washington was so far from the Rocky Mountains, that he wished to get a horse to ride back. They all looked very cunning and shrewd. They belonged to entirely savage tribes, not yet settled in the "Indian territory;" but were the original owners of their hunting-grounds.

The "great father" told them that the Indian agent of the Government would take care of them, and instruct them in the art of tilling the ground, and raising abundant food, of weaving their cloathes, and manufacturing their tools; he intimated to one of them that the United States would probably treat with his nation for the cession of a strip of land for a road; and he promised to the other that they should return on iron horses, much swifter than any living horse could carry them.

After all, the Indians seemed pretty well comforted by receiving silver medals, and a larger star-spangled flag. As the squaws were unexpected visitors, Mrs. Fillmore had nothing to give them but sugar-plums.

I cannot accustom myself to the Western fare in the hotels and on the boats. . . . Even the water looks unpalatable; it is the Mississippi water, with all the mud of its bottoms dissolved by the melting snow.

"How do you like America, sir? Is it not a great country?" said a gentleman to Mr. Pulszky.

"Of course it is," was the answer.

"Have you found anything here which fell short of your expectation?"

"Your political institutions are admirable," replied Mr Pulszky; "your people are enterprising and energetic; but, after all, there is nothing perfect under the sun."

"Well, sir, what can you object to?" continued the American, a planter, who probably wished to open thus a discussion on slavery. Mr. Pulszky took up his glass, and said:

"For instance, I object to the mud in the Mississippi water which you drink."

"Sir," retorted the American, "it has been chemically analysed and compared with the waters of other rivers, and it was ascertained that the Ganges as well as the Nile contain several per cents more of animal matter than the Mississippi."

"I have every regard for the sacred rivers of the Hindoos and the Egyptians," said Mr. Pulszky; "yet I am ready to give the palm to your father of rivers. Only I do not see why the mud of the Himalaya and the Abyssinian mountains should justify you in drinking the mud of the Western prairie. Don't you know here the use of filters?"

"Sir," exclaimed the American, indignantly, "how should we not?"

"Then why do you not filter your water?" asked Mr. Pulszky.

Without hesitating one moment, the planter replied: "We are such a *go-a-head people* that we have no time to filter our water."

After their trip to America the Pulszkys went to Italy, where they joined Garibaldi's struggle for Italian independence. In 1866 a pardon from Vienna allowed them to return to Hungary. Pulszky was later made director of state museums and libraries. Kossuth, however, spent the rest of his life in exile, first in England, then in Italy.

Francis and Theresa Pulszky, White Red Black. Sketches of Society in the United States During the Visit of Their Guest. *Trubner, 1853; reprinted, Negro Universities Press, 1968. The sections quoted are described as "From Mrs. Pulszky's Diary." Vol. I, 194–98, 225–27, 229–31; II, 232–33.*

11

Marianne Finch on Women and Slaves

Marianne Finch came to America from England in 1850 especially for the purpose of attending a Woman's Rights Convention, and stayed through most of 1850 and 1851.

During the winter of 1851 there were two or three texts that seemed especial favourites with many of the American divines, viz.:—

"Servants be obedient to your masters."

"Wives submit yourselves to your husbands."

"Let your women learn in silence."

These watchful shepherds apprehended danger to their flocks from the passing of the Fugitive Slave Bill, and the holding of the Woman's Convention in the autumn of that year. And most earnestly and eloquently did they exhort their hearers to uphold the majesty of the law, and the Divine right of man—(if he were white)—against the machinations of slaves and women.

I remember one of these sermons was quite a masterpiece; and proved to the satisfaction of every one—unless it were a fugitive slave (who, of course, is incapable of reasoning on the subject)—that it was the duty of every fugitive slave to give himself up.

From these reverend gentlemen I received much new light on the subject of feminine and slave virtue.

In a paper edited by one of them, a leading divine of New York, in replying to a correspondent, he strenuously opposes women taking part in anything public, overwhelming all opposition with this astounding climax—"Place woman unbonneted and unshawled before the public gaze, and what becomes of her modesty and virtue!" What, indeed, if it be all in her bonnet and shawl?

How destitute our fashionable ladies must be of these invaluable qualities who constantly appear before "the public gaze" at balls, operas, concerts, theatres, not only without bonnets and shawls; but, in their struggles to be fully dressed without these essentials to female virtue, do sometimes contrive to undress themselves beyond the confines of health and decency. I wonder what has become of the *modesty* and *virtue* of Jenny Lind, whose voice rose higher than any in the States, and who never appeared in public without being "unbonneted and unshawled" for the express purpose of being gazed at and listened to by admiring thousands.

From these discourses I learnt that the same arguments were used against the claims of the women as against those of the slaves; and that their cases had many points of resemblance.

In the first place the virtues most required in women and slaves are the same, namely, humility, obedience, submission to authority. The thing condemned in both is, a love of freedom—a desire to enlarge their field of action—to increase their sources of information.

The comparison holds good in other respects—for instance, a man marries a woman—*he gives her his name*; in return the *law gives him her person*, her property, her children, her earnings, and everything that is hers.

The law is equally liberal to the owner of the slave; the chief difference being that the latter costs from 50£ to 150£, while the wife may be had for nothing.

They are alike excluded from all share in the government;—they are both amenable to laws, in the making of which they have had no share, and which, as far as they are concerned, are partial and unjust.

The education and employment of both, however varied, are

limited to the tastes and wants of their proprietors, for whose pleasure and use it is supposed they were created.

All this I learnt from eminent divines and others who zealously upheld what was *lawful,* and frequently opposed what was *just.* Besides which, I received many fancy sketches of those monstrous women who met at Worcester to talk about their rights and wrongs.

In spite of myself I found their president (Mrs. Paulina Davis) fixed in my mind, as a coarse, masculine, overbearing, disagreeable person; with a dirty house, a neglected family, and a hen-pecked husband. Being unexpectedly introduced to her, I was as much puzzled as we are told Napoleon was, when he had to deal with an honest man,—for any other kind he was prepared; *I was prepared* for anything monstrous, but to find Mrs. Davis, a fair, delicate-looking woman, with gentle manners, and a low voice, which she uses sparingly, completely set at nought all my pre-conceived notions.

I afterwards visited her at her home, near Providence, where I remained with her several days. Here again my fancy portrait was all wrong;—I found her a deeply-loved, and most affectionate wife; an excellent housekeeper, and an indefatigable needle-woman. Had I not witnessed her home-virtues, I confess myself sufficiently prejudiced to have overlooked her public services. But having satisfied myself that she was regular in her devotions at the altar of the household gods, I felt at liberty to admire the clear intelligence by which she saw the bearings of this woman's movement, and deeply respected the courage and generosity that induced her to throw herself into it, and incur the responsibility and odium of leadership, during its infancy and unpopularity.

I asked her how it happened that, being so happy in her domestic relations, and surrounded by all the comforts and so many of the elegances of life, she should take so deep an interest in this unprecedented movement?

She replied, "because she saw in *this movement* what she found in *no other*—the means of rendering woman useful and happy to the extent of her nature."

Her *faith was firm*, because it was *founded on knowledge* gained from *her own experience*.

With an active mind, the first eighteen years of her life were spent under circumstances of great restraint, to which she attributes in a great measure the extreme delicacy of her health. She then married, attended to her housekeeping, mended stockings, and sewed on buttons duly, and "subjected herself to her own husband in everything."

This did pretty well with a good husband and a good income, but suddenly the former died, leaving his affairs (of which she was kept in entire ignorance) very much involved, and she found herself not only deprived of her husband and her means of living, but surrounded by debt and difficulty.

What was she to do? Her capacity for housekeeping and stocking-mending availed her nothing, they had not prevented the calamity, neither would they help her out of it. She had the choice of other women similarly circumstanced—teaching, sewing, serving, or starving—to all these she objected.

It happened that in the course of her reading she had met with "Combe's Constitution of Man," a book which not only added to her love of the study of physiology, but strongly impressed her with a sense of its importance, especially to women, who, generally speaking, know so little about it. With this conviction she determined to educate herself for a lecturer on the subject.

Accordingly she proceeded to New York, and now it was that she realized all the difficulties and annoyances that were thrown in her path merely on account of her sex. Colleges were closed against her; books and apparatus were denied her; professors could not receive her with their pupils: however she persevered, sometimes stealing her knowledge by inducing doorkeepers and librarians to allow her to lock herself up with the manikins, skeletons, books, and other treasures entrusted to their keeping. At other times receiving her lessons at five o'clock in the morning, that she might not interfere with the students of the more privileged sex.

After passing through this she had to go through another

ordeal, to establish herself as a lecturer. In this also she succeeded, as well as in making it remunerative.

After several years spent in this way, in which she says she learnt more than she could have done in a century from her former mode of life, she met with her present husband, a most worthy man, of whose intelligence and liberality it is superfluous to speak, since it is sufficiently proved by his choosing her for a wife, and their mutual attachment. . . .

Subsequently I became acquainted with many of both sexes connected with this movement. I found they varied in circumstances, education, religion, and even in politics, but all united in an earnest protest against slavery in every form, whether of sex or colour, direct or indirect. They were earnest, intelligent, deep-thinking men and women, and the speeches delivered and the resolutions passed at their last convention, contained in a report now lying before me, corroborate this statement.

Finch met other women lecturers of the day, including Delia Bacon, who gave well-attended lectures on literature, art, and history, and Harriot Hunt, a practicing physician although she had not been allowed to attend professional classes. (Fredrika Bremer also spoke of Harriot Hunt. See page 68, above.) Finch also met Dr. Emily Blackwell, sister of Dr. Elizabeth Blackwell, the first American women graduated from an established medical school.

On her return to England, Finch was pleased to find that something had been done at home to increase the industrial resources of women, namely, the organization of a Ladies' Guild to educate women to become self-supporting.

Marianne Finch, An Englishwoman's Experience in America. *London: Richard Bentley, 1853; reprinted, Negro Universities Press, 1969. Pages 204–214.*

12

Ida Pfeiffer Visits California Indians

Ida Reyer Pfeiffer (1797–1858), a Viennese housewife, waited until her sons were grown to indulge a passion for travel. She circled the globe in 1846–1848, and in 1853 came to California on her return from a second journey around the world.

SEPTEMBER 25, 1853

At length . . . sounded the long-desired cry of "Land! land!" and in the evening the coast of California lay spread out before our eyes. And yet, though I had now been three months in the saline prison, and for more than two had seen no land, this coast did not make a pleasing impression on me, but, on the contrary, rather a melancholy one. It was, beyond all description, desolate and dead. Naked sand-hills rose steeply on all sides. No tree, no shrub, not so much as a blade of grass, varied the melancholy color of the corpse-like waste.

And to this desert men voluntarily banish themselves for the chance of finding a lump of gold! What must a place be, if it had but this attraction, to keep off the avaricious whites?

I made three excursions from San Francisco to the interior of California; the first to Sacramento, Marysville, and the gold-mines of the Yuba river; the second to Crescent City and the Rogue-river Indians; and the third to St. José. . . .

At Marysville . . . I was most interested by the natives, who are of pure Indian descent, and have preserved themselves from any mixture of Spanish blood. These savages, as we call them, are diminishing from year to year, under the pressure of the hard, encroaching whites. . . .

These people stand on a very low grade of civilization. They neither till the ground, nor keep cattle, nor hunt—do nothing, in short, but fish; and for their dwellings, they dig in the ground holes of eighteen or twenty feet long, and two feet deep, over which they put a roof, of a tent-like shape, made of wood and clay. The door to these habitations is a small hole, through which you must creep on hands and knees; and a still smaller opening in the roof lets the smoke out.

They have neither mats nor earthen vessels, and they understand no work but basket plaiting. In this art, however, they have attained to great perfection; they know how to make their baskets perfectly water-tight, and manage even to boil their fish in them. They plait large baskets to keep their dried fish in, smaller to fetch water, and quite little ones that they put on their heads as hats.

It was toward evening when I visited this tribe, and the people were sitting before their holes, by small fires, preparing and eating their evening meal, which consisted of broiled fish and acorn bread. The last-named article is very solid, heavy, and damp, and has rather a bitter taste. They make it by pounding the acorns to power; and with this they make bread without mixing in any thing else than water. Besides fish and acorns, they eat pretty nearly every thing else that they can get at— frogs, squirrels, grasshoppers, and beetles, which last are considered as dainties.

I saw among these poor creatures many who were ill of fever, some insane, and astonishingly few children. The Indians who live in the neighborhood of the whites are said to die off much more rapidly than those who have taken refuge in the interior of the forests. The former obtain, in exchange for their fish and other little articles of trade, chiefly spirituous liquors, which is poison to them, constantly making them ill, and frequently killing them outright. Another cause of terrible mortality among them is the small-pox, a disease which they have also received from their white neighbors.

CRESCENT CITY

The chief purpose of my coming had been to visit the Indians, who are still to be found in great numbers in this part of California; but they are retiring further and further into the interior. . . . To proceed with safety into the country as far as the Rogue [River] Indians on the Smith's River, it was necessary, I was told, to go in armed company, as these Indians are very savage and cunning.

Mrs. Pfeiffer had just come from visiting headhunting tribes of Borneo, and had no fear of the natives of the Pacific coast. She accepted the offer of a German sailor, who had traded with the Indians and understood their language, to serve as her guide.

NOVEMBER 7

We went about sixteen miles, mostly along the sea-shore, through deep sand or over stones. Through the forests the paths were good, and when, toward the afternoon, we took a turn inland we soon arrived at Smith's River, the banks of which are entirely of sand; but about half a mile into the country begin some magnificent pine woods. . . .

We passed several villages, but made a very short stay, in order to reach, if possible, a shelter for the night before the rain set in, as it threatened to do soon. They were very small, consisting of not more than seven or eight wigwams or holes, like those of Marysville, except that the wooden framework of the roof was here covered with leaves and branches instead of clay.

We crossed Smith's River in the hollowed trunk of a tree, and the people made use of a quite heavy plank for a rudder.

The further we went from the settlements of the whites the less and less were the people clothed; and at length they appeared in a complete state of nature, excepting only a kind of apology for an apron, worn by the women, sometimes made of elk's skin and sometimes of grass; but the skin was cut up into narrow strips, leaving only a piece of about three inches broad whole at the top. They wind this kind of fringe twice round them, and it looks like a piece of very ragged fur. I saw it even on the smallest girls, who could scarcely walk. Some of the chiefs had a skin flung like a mantle over their shoulders.

Toward evening we reached a great village, the inhabitants of which call themselves *Huna* Indians. My companion had never been so far before; but he knew one young man among them, with whom he had had dealings for fish and beads, and we determined to pass the night here. It began to rain again, and the cold was so excessive that I was glad to find a place in one of these earth-holes, in the midst of the disgusting naked natives.

We lay down round the fire, which blazed up merrily in the middle of the hut, and about which half a dozen Indians were already crouching; but the hut soon became filled to overflowing with curious visitors, and the heat and vapors so suffocating that I was driven out again in despair, thinking I should prefer the rain and the cold.

It was not, however, from rain and cold only that I had to suffer; for the whole population of the village thronged about me, and formed a small close circle, so that I could hardly move. They pulled me this way and that; examined every article of my clothing from my hat to my shoes; and once even dragged me away to some remote huts in the forest, so that I found some difficulty in getting back to that of my host.

I had some bread and cheese, and my companion had brought with him sugar, coffee, and bread, and also a little tin kettle, in which he made some coffee, as he called it, though there was hardly enough coffee to tinge the water. But the hot drink was, nevertheless, most highly approved of. The kettle was soon emptied and a second edition called for; and when the Indians saw that he put in a little brown powder, they wanted to have some of that, and seized on it to eat it. The sugar they did not put into the coffee, but ate it eagerly alone, as well as the bread, and we had no peace till it was all gone. My guide was not able to save any of his provisions for the following morning.

After this meal was over the Indians set about their own cooking. They brought out some large, fine salmon, with which the waters of California abound; cut off the head and tail, split up the fish, and stuck in splinters of wood to keep it open, and then put it on a large wooden spit and roasted it before the fire.

Of the heads and tails they made a kind of soup. They filled one of their close baskets with water, and threw in red-hot stones, which they continually replaced with fresh ones, till the water began to simmer, and then they put in the heads and tails of the fish and let them boil. In a short time the water had thickened and become of a grayish color, perhaps because a good quantity of ashes had gone in with the hot stones; but the people were not very exact in these matters.

The soup they ate with shells; the roasted fish they tore to pieces with their hands, and laid upon flat baskets that serve them for plates. After this they roasted the acorns in the hot ashes, and ate with a long thin grass root by way of dessert. These last were not only raw but unwashed, with the earth still sticking about them; but they had an extremely delicious taste, and were so soft that they could be mashed with the tongue. The meal was abundant, and would have been excellent if it had only been flavored with salt and—cleanliness; but both the one and the other are unknown to these people.

After supper the gentlemen, young and old, made their toilet, by daubing their faces in a most detestable manner with red, blue, or black paint. They first smeared them with fish fat, and then they rubbed in the paint, sometimes passing a finger over it in certain lines, so as to produce a pattern, and it is hardly necessary to say that their natural ugliness was greatly increased by the pains they had taken to adorn themselves.

When they had concluded this operation they began to sing, and their songs were really more melodious and better sung than I could have expected from such a rude people. The entertainment was prolonged till a late hour in the night, and then they were so polite as to leave the hole to me, in so far that the men went away and only the women remained near me. One of them placed herself so close on one side of me, that I could hardly turn round; and on the other side, close to me, stood a large basket containing smoked fish; overhead hung another basket of fish to be smoked; and we lay on the bare cold ground, without pillow or covering, so it may be imagined what a luxurious night I passed.

I had taken very little of the supper, but had a private intention of making myself amends afterward by having some bread and cheese when every body else was asleep; but I did not dare produce such dainties as long as the people were about, for every body would have wanted to taste, and at last there would have been nothing left for me. When the women were all asleep, that is snoring, I raised myself up a little, and very cautiously drew forth my treasure. But my next neighbor either slept very lightly, or had only been pretending to be asleep; for she sat up instantly and asked me what I was doing, signifying to me that I was to lie down and not move. She then kept stirring the fire until I stretched myself out again and pretended to fall asleep, when she lay down once more at my side. Probably they felt some sort of mistrust of me.

NOVEMBER 8

After breakfast we continued our journey, and traveled this day seventeen or eighteen miles, entirely through magnificent woods. When we had proceeded but a short distance we came upon the Oregon Territory, and soon met with a tribe of the Rogue-river Indians. We entered several of the wigwams, and my guide tried to get some fish, which he had not hitherto been able to do; and I crept, as I had done the day before, into many of these earthy habitations, to observe the mode of life and doings of the people.

The Indians of the North of California stand at the very lowest point of culture, and are said to have no idea of religion or of a future state; but in many of their villages you find a sort of conjuror or "medicine man" who undertakes by his potent art to cure diseases, discover thefts, and point out the places where stolen goods lie concealed.

These Indians do not scalp their enemies or take them prisoners, but they kill all the men who fall into their power, though never the women. If a woman or a child comes within range of their arrows, they call to them to get out of the way. They fight with men, they say, and not with the weak and helpless—an example that may make us feel ashamed when we remember in how many of the wars of whites women and children have been tortured and murdered. . . .

These Indians are represented as treacherous, cowardly, and revengeful, and only attacking the whites when they find one alone. But, after all, what other means of attack have they against the well-armed whites—the domineering race from which they have had so much to suffer. Revenge is really natural to man; and if the whites had suffered as many wrongs from them as they from the whites, I rather think they too would have felt the desire of revenge.

NOVEMBER 10

I found myself once more in Crescent City, and bringing with me a very painful impression of the lot of the poor driven-out Indians. . . . The great fault of the government is over-indulgence toward the white settlers, mostly men almost as rude as the savages themselves, and far less well disposed, who shamefully abuse the indulgence. As long as there are so few courts of justice in the country that it is very difficult for a native to find his way to one, and until these courts show some more just severity to the misconduct of the settlers, the poor Indian will remain the sport of the insolent white.

Mrs. Pfeiffer went on to Panama and South America before return-ing to the United States, then to London, which she reached in June 1855; her last journey was to Madagascar, where she suffered such hardships that she died soon after reaching home in 1858.

Ida Reyer Pfeiffer, A Lady's Second Journey Round the World. *New York: Harper, 1856. Pages 288, 300, 306–8, 312, 313–17, 319, 321–22. A part was also published as* A Lady's Visit to California, 1853. *Oakland, Calif.: Biobooks, 1950.*

13

Isabella Bird Rides the Cars

Isabella Lucy Bird (1831–1904) came from England to America in 1854, as she said, "with that amount of prejudice which seems the birthright of every English person," but as she traveled across the country she found that prejudice melting away. She had been advised to travel by her doctor, for she had always been frail and sickly. Surprisingly, all her health problems also melted away the farther she got from her native soil.

1854

At half past three we entered the cars in a long shed, where there were no officials in uniform as in England, and we found our way in as we could. "All aboard!" is the signal for taking places, but on this occasion a loud shout of "Tumble in for your lives!" greeted by amused ears, succeeded by "Go-ahead!" and off we went, the engineer tolling a heavy bell to notify our approach to the passengers in *the streets along which we passed.* America has certainly flourished under her motto "Go a-head!" but the cautious "All right!" of an English guard, who waits to start till he is sure of his ground being clear, gives one more confidence.

I never experienced the same amount of fear which is expressed by *Bunn* and other writers, for, on comparing the number of accidents with the number of miles of railway open in America, I did not find the disadvantage in point of safety on her side.

The cars are a complete novelty to an English eye. They are twenty-five feet long, and hold about sixty persons; they have twelve windows on either side, and two and a door at each end; a passage runs down the middle, with chairs to hold two each on either side. There is a small saloon for ladies with babies at one end, and a filter containing a constant supply of iced water. There are rings along the roof for a rope which passes through each car to the engine, so that anything wrong can be communicated instantly to the engineer. Every car has eight solid wheels, four being placed close together at each end, all of which can be locked by two powerful breaks [sic].

At each end of every car is a platform, and passengers are "prohibited from standing upon it at their peril," as also from passing from car to car while the train is in motion; but as no penalty attaches to this law, it is incessantly and continuously violated, "free and enlightened citizens" being at perfect liberty to imperil their own necks; and "poor, ignorant, benighted Britishers" soon learn to follow their example. Persons are for ever passing backwards and forwards, exclusive of the conductor whose business it is, and water-carriers, book, bonbon, and peach vendors.

No person connected with these railways wears a distinguishing dress, and the stations, or "depôts" as they are called, are generally of the meanest description, mere wooden sheds, with a ticket-office very difficult to discover. If you are so fortunate as to find a man standing at the door of the baggage-car, he attaches copper plates to your trunks, with a number and the name of the place you are going to upon them, giving you labels with corresponding numbers. By this excellent arrangement, in going a very long journey, in which you are obliged to change cars several times, and cross rivers and lakes in steamers, you are relieved of all responsibility, and only require at the end to give your checks to the hotel-porter, who regains your baggage without any trouble on your part.

This plan would be worthily imitated at our termini in England, where I have frequently seen "unprotected females" in the last stage of frenzy at being pushed out of the way, while some persons unknown are running off with their possessions.

When you reach a *depôt*, as there are no railway porters, numerous men clamour to take your effects to an hotel, but, as many of these are thieves, it is necessary to be very careful in only selecting those who have hotel-badges on their hats.

An emigrant-car is attached to each train, but there is only one class: thus it may happen that you have on one side the President of the Great Republic, and on the other the *gentleman* who blacked your shoes in the morning. The Americans, however, have too much respect for themselves and their companions to travel except in good clothes, and this mingling of all ranks is far from being disagreeable, particularly to a stranger like myself, one of whose objects was to see things in their everyday dress. We must be well aware that in many parts of England it would be difficult for a lady to travel unattended in a second-class, impossible in a third-class carriage; yet I have travelled several thousand miles in America, frequently alone, from the house of one friend to another's, and never met with anything approaching to incivility; and I have often heard it stated that a lady, no matter what her youth or attractions might be, could travel alone through every State in the Union, and never meet with anything but attention and respect.

I have had considerable experience of the cars, having travelled from the Atlantic to the Mississippi, and from the Mississippi to the St. Lawrence, and found the company so agreeable in its way, and the cars themselves so easy, well ventilated, and comfortable, that, were it not for the disgusting practice of spitting upon the floors in which the lower classes of Americans indulge, I should greatly prefer them to our own exclusive carriages, denominated in the States "'*coon sentry-boxes.*"

Well, we are seated in the cars; a man shouts "Go-ahead!" and we are off, the engine ringing its heavy bell, and thus began my experiences of American travel.

What strange people now crammed the cars! Traders, merchants, hunters, diggers, trappers, and adventurers from every land, most of them armed to the teeth, and not without good reason; for within the last few months, Indians, enraged at the aggressions of the white men, have taken a terrible revenge upon western travellers.

Some of their rifles were of most costly workmanship, and were nursed with paternal care by their possessors. On the seat in front of me were two "prairie-men," such as are described in the 'Scalp-Hunters,' though of an inferior grade to St. Vrain. Fine specimens of men they were; tall, handsome, broad-chested, and athletic, with aquiline noses, piercing grey eyes, and brown curling hair and beards. They wore leathern jackets, slashed and embroidered, leather smallclothes, large boots with embroidered tops, silver spurs, and caps of scarlet cloth, worked with somewhat tarnished gold thread, doubtless the gifts of some fair ones enamoured of the handsome physiognomies and reckless bearing of the hunters.

Dulness fled from their presence; they could tell stories, whistle melodies, and sing comic songs without weariness or cessation; fortunate were those near enough to be enlivened by their drolleries during the tedium of a night detention. Each of them wore a leathern belt—with two pistols stuck into it—gold earrings, and costly rings. Blithe, cheerful souls they were, telling racy stories of Western life, chivalrous in their manners, and free as the winds.

There were Californians dressed for the diggings, with leather pouches for the gold-dust; Mormons on their way to Utah; and restless spirits seeking for that excitement and variety which they had sought for in vain in civilized life! And conveying this motley assortment of human beings, the cars dashed along.

Cincinnati is famous for its public libraries and reading-rooms. The Young Men's Mercantile Library Association has a very handsome suite of rooms opened as libraries and reading-rooms, the number of books amounting to 16,000, these, with upwards of 100 newspapers, being well selected by a managing committee; none of our English works of good repute being awanting. The facility with which English books are reprinted in America, and the immense circulation which they attain in consequence of their cheapness, greatly increases the responsibility which rests upon our authors as to the direction which they give, whether for good or evil, to the intelligent and inquiring minds of the youth of America—minds ceaselessly occupied, both in religion and politics, in investigation and inquiry—in overturning old systems before they have devised new ones. . . .

But after describing the beauty of her streets, her astonishing progress, and the splendour of her shops, I must not close this chapter without stating that the Queen City bears the less elegant name of Porkopolis; that swine, lean, gaunt, and vicious-looking, riot through her streets; and that, on coming out of the most splendid stores, one stumbles over these disgusting intruders. Cincinnati is the city of pigs. As there is a railway system and a hotel system, so there is also a *pig system*, by which this place is marked out from any other.

Huge quantities of these useful animals are reared after harvest in the corn-fields of Ohio, and on the beech-mast and acorns of its gigantic forests. At a particular time of year they arrive by thousands—brought in droves and steamers to the number of 500,000—to meet their doom, when it is said that the Ohio runs red with blood! There are huge slaughter-houses behind the town, something on the plan of the *abattoirs* of Paris—large wooden buildings, with numerous pens, from whence the pigs march in single file along a narrow passage, to an apartment where each, on his entrance, receives a blow with a hammer, which deprives him of consciousness, and in a short time, by means of numerous hands, and a well-managed caldron system, he is cut up ready for pickling. . . .

At one establishment 12,000 pigs are killed, pickled, and packed every fall; and in the whole neighbourhood, as I have heard in the cars, the "hog crop" is as much a subject of discussion and speculation as the cotton crop of Alabama, the hop-picking of Kent, or the harvest in England.

Kentucky, the land, by reputation, of "red horses, bowie-knives, and gouging," is only separated from Ohio by the river Ohio; and on a day when the thermometer stood at 103° in the shade I went to the town of Covington. Marked, wide, and almost inestimable, is the difference between the free state of Ohio and the slave-state of Kentucky. They have the same soil, the same climate, and precisely the same natural advantages; yet the total absence of progress, if not the appearance of retrogression and decay, the loungers in the streets, and the peculiar appearance of the slaves, afford a contrast to the bustle on the opposite side of the river, which would strike the most unobservant.

I was credibly informed that property of the same value was worth 300 dollars in Kentucky and 3000 in Ohio! Free emigrants and workmen will not settle in Kentucky, where they would be brought into contact with compulsory slave-labour; thus the development of industry is retarded, and the difference will become more apparent every year, till possibly some great changes will be forced upon the legislature.

Few English people will forget the impression made upon them by the first sight of a slave—a being created in the image of God, yet the *bona fide* property of his fellow-man. The first I saw was an African female, the slave of a lady from Florida, with a complexion black as the law which held her in captivity.

The subject of slavery is one which has lately been brought so prominently before the British people by Mrs. Beecher Stowe, that I shall be pardoned for making a few remarks upon it. Powerfully written as the book is, and much as I admire the benevolent intentions of the writer, I am told that the effect of the volume has been prejudicial, and this assertion is borne out by persons well acquainted with the subject in the free states. A gentleman very eminent in his country, as having devoted himself from his youth to the cause of abolition, as a steadfast pursuer of one grand principle, together with other persons, say that " 'Uncle Tom's Cabin' had thrown the cause back for many years!"

An unexceptional censure ought not to be pronounced without a more complete knowledge of the subject than can be gained from novels and newspapers; still less ought this censure to extend to America as a whole, for the people of the Northern States are more ardent abolitionists than ourselves—more consistent, in fact, for they have no white slaves, no oppressed factory children, the cry of whose wrongs ascends daily into the ears of an avenging judge. Still, blame must attach to *them* for the way in which they place the coloured people in an inferior social position, a rigid system of exclusiveness shutting them out from the usual places of amusement and education.

It must not be forgotten that England bequeathed this system to her colonies, though she has nobly blotted it out from those which still own her sway; that it is encouraged by the cotton lords of Preston and Manchester; and that the great measure of negro emancipation was carried, not by the violent declamation and ignorant railings of men who sought popularity by exciting the passions of the multitude, but by the persevering exertions and practical Christian philanthropy of Mr. [William] Wilberforce and his coadjutors.

It is naturally to be expected that a person writing a book on America would offer some remarks upon this subject, and raise a voice, however feeble, against so gigantic an evil. The conclusions which I have stated in the foregoing pages are derived from a careful comparison and study of facts which I have learned from eminent speakers and writers both in favour of and against the slave-system.

Miss Bird again visited the United States in 1873, on her way home from a visit to the Sandwich Islands. Completely restored to health and an experienced traveler, she crossed the country from west to east (see pages 125–32).

[Isabella Bird] The Englishwoman in America. *London: Murray, 1856. Pages 92–95, 140–41, 124–27, 131-32.*

14

Amelia Murray on the American Character and Slavery

The Honorable Amelia Matilda Murray (1795–1888) was a daughter of Lord George Murray, Bishop of St. David's. She was a Lady of the Bedchamber to Queen Victoria. An amateur botanist, she came to America to study the plants of the New World. As she traveled throughout the eastern states in 1854 and 1855, she sketched many plants and scenes. Her nephew, the Honorable Charles Augustus Murray, had "done" the United States in 1834–1836.

NEWPORT, RHODE ISLAND, 1854

We drove by Newport to the bathing sands, where gentlemen take charge of ladies in the surf: it was to me a very singular and amusing scene—numerous carriages, drawn up before a semicircle of small bathing-houses, containing gaily dressed occupants, who had taken their marine walk, or were waiting for the ladies, young and old, still frolicking about among the waves, children dancing in and out, gentlemen handling about their pretty partners as if they were dancing water quadrilles, and heads, young and old, with streaming hair dipping in and out: it was very droll, very lively, and I daresay very amusing to all engaged.

No accident has ever occurred here, for the bay is protected

98

by capes on each side, and the water is shallow for some distance out. A white flag is raised during the hours appropriated to ladies, and it is succeeded by a red one, later in the day, when gentlemen take possession of the shore on their own account. The scene resembled that on a racecourse in England. I made a slight sketch from the hill above; it was unique in its way, for I believe there are few places, even in America, where the sea would be safe for such an experiment: and even here the aid of strong arms is at times very necessary to save ladies from being knocked over by the waves. There was considerable surf to-day, but, from the numbers who breasted it, I suppose the courage necessary for the undertaking is not so great as it appears to me. I should look on a long while before I could try this kind of experiment.

WASHINGTON

By promoting healthier ideas upon education, the crude and absurd opinions too generally advanced and acted upon, will be amended and counteracted, and an improved and more practical female training will be encouraged. It will no longer be gravely enunciated at an educational convention—'That the stimulus which the human heart requires is wanting for women in the present age, and that society gives them nothing to aim at;' but if so, give them reasonable aims.

Let them aim at duty, not notoriety. Let them keep within their appropriate sphere, cultivating sufficient moral courage to act within that sphere for the benefit of their fellow-creatures, and particularly for the advantage of their sex; disciplining and training their own minds to be the educated companions, not the rivals, of men. Let them be the heart-consolers, the binders-up of broken spirits, the 'sisters of the sisterless,' the presiding geniuses of the social circle. Is that not work enough for them to do?

In this country, I hear that 'though it has no queen, *all the women are queens.*' I should rather call them playthings—dolls; things treated as if they were unfit or unwilling to help themselves or others; and while we in England have nearly cast aside arts of the toilet worthy only of dolls, I see here false brows, false blooms, false hair, false everything!—not always, but too frequently. Dress in America, as an almost general rule, is full of extravagance and artificiality; and while women show such a want of reliance upon their native powers of pleasing, their influence in society will be more nominal than real.

CHARLESTON, SOUTH CAROLINA, JANUARY 7, 1855

I begin to mark cotton plantations, and my compassionate feelings are rapidly changing sides. It appears to me our benevolent intentions in England have taken a mistaken direction, and that we should bestow our compassion on the masters instead of on the slaves. The former by no means enjoy the incubus with which circumstances have loaded them, and would be only too happy if they could supersede this black labour by white; but as to the negroes, they are the merriest, most contented set of people I ever saw; of course there are exceptions, but I am inclined to suspect that we have as much vice, and more suffering, than is caused here by the unfortunate institution of Slavery; and I very much doubt if freedom will ever make the black population, in the mass, anything more than a set of grown-up children.

Even as to the matter of purchase and sale, it is disliked by masters; and I find compassion very much wasted upon the objects of it. An old lady died here lately, and her negroes were to be parted with; Mrs. S——, an acquaintance of mine, knew these blacks, and shed tears about their change of fate; but when they came to market, and she found all so gay and indifferent about it, she could not help feeling her sorrow was greatly thrown away.

Mrs. [Harriet Beecher] Stowe's Topsy is a perfect illustration of Darkie's character, and many of the sad histories of which her book is made up may be true as isolated facts; but yet I feel sure that, as a whole, the story, however ingeniously worked up, is an unfair picture; a libel upon the slaveholders as a body. I very much doubt if a real Uncle Tom can often be found in the whole negro race; and if such a being is, or was, he is as great a rarity as a Shakespeare among whites.

One particular want appears to me evident in negro minds and character: they have no consciousness of the fitness of things. I suffer now from the cold wintry weather here; and upon my begging Blackie for a better fire in my room, in the civilest, most anxious tone, he asked whether I would not like some iced water? . . .

I begin to doubt whether they ever grow mentally after twenty. They are precocious children, being so imitative; they soon ripen, come to a stand-still, and advance no farther. In this respect Uncle Tom is a myth, but Topsy a reality.

I mean to go and see a sale of slaves; my wish is to judge the subject fairly in all its bearings, and this I may be trusted to do even by Abolitionists; for early prejudices and my national and acquired feelings are certainly opposed to slavery; but if countenances are 'a history as well as a prophecy,' the national expression of faces in the North as contrasted with those of the South tell a strange, and to me an unexpected story, as regards the greatest happiness principle of the greatest number!

Of course, it must be borne in mind that no rules are without exception; but, oh, the haggard, anxious, melancholy, restless, sickly, hopeless faces I have seen in the Northern States—in the rail-cars, on the steam-boats, in the saloons, and particularly in the ladies' parlour. There is beauty of feature and complexion, with hardly any individuality of character. Nothing like simplicity, even among children after ten years of age—hot-house, forced impetuous beings, the *almighty dollars*, the incentive and only guide to activity and appreciation. Women care that their husbands should gain gold, that they may spend it in dress and ostentation; and the men like that their wives should appear as queens, whether they rule well, or ill, or at all; yet it is certain that I have made the acquaintance, and that I value the friendship, of superior women in the North, and if I should be thought to have expressed myself with too much severity, I appeal to their candour and judgment; and being American cousins they have the Anglo-Saxon love of Truth, and will not spurn her even in an unveiled form, or receive her ungraciously even when thus presented. I have reason to speak gratefully, and warmly do I feel, and anxiously do I venture these observations, which may seem even harsh and ungrateful.

I do not yet know much of the Southern ladies; but from Washington to this place I have been struck by a general improvement of countenance and manner in the white race, and this in spite of the horrors which accompany the misuse of tobacco. If the gentlemen of this part of the country would only acquire habits of self-control and decency in this matter, they would indeed become the *Preux Chevaliers* of the United States, as their hills and valleys may prove the store-houses and gardens of the Union. May their sons and daughters look to these things, and increase in wealth, prosperity, virtue, and happiness!

Murray added an epilogue to her book critical of the philanthropists of Great Britain for their stand against slavery. This led to her retirement as Lady of the Bedchamber, since members of the Court were not allowed to publish political views. She afterwards supported female education and "ragged schools" for destitute children.

Amelia M. Murray, Letters from the United States, Cuba and Canada. *New York: Putnam, 1856; reprinted, Negro Universities Press, 1969. Pages 32, 174–75, 197–200.*

15

Maria Theresa Longworth Visits Celebrated Sites

Maria Theresa Longworth (1832?–1881) was a controversial figure in Great Britain. Because she was a Catholic and Major William Yelverton, whom she married in 1857, was a Protestant, the marriage was declared illegal. Despite the facts that he had deserted her and married another woman, Theresa spent many years in litigation to establish her conjugal rights and continued to uphold her right to her husband's name. After the major's father died in 1870, he had the right of succession to the title of Viscount Avonmore, and she assumed the title of Viscountess Avonmore. Her visit to America took place in the early 1870s. Her account gives no dates of arrival or departure.

The author of the following sketches has travelled twenty thousand miles through the most important districts of America, with the one object of seeing the country and understanding the people. She has visited most of the largest cities, and has known, and had favourable opportunities of conversing with, their leading inhabitants.

CHATTANOOGA, TENNESSEE

In a wide, bare, woodless valley—now of some historical interest, from the many battles fought there during the "War of Secession"—lies the town of Chattanooga, Tennessee. The houses are so scattered, that they look as if sprinkled over the vast plain. There are no regularly planned streets, each person would seem to have made his own road, or pathway, in whatever direction best pleased him.

The town has a general appearance of having been tossed there by accident, or of having slipped from the mountains in a storm of bricks and wooden huts.

The valley extends for eighteen miles, and is surrounded by several ranges of mountains, rising one above another, the only exit appearing to be where the Tennessee river flows beneath the foot of Lookout Mountain. This valley of Chattanooga is one of the most celebrated sites in the United States, and to my mind, the most beautiful of any I had then seen. We procured a carriage to take us to the top of the mountain, to the hotel called the "Mountain House." As we ascended the mountain— which rises two thousand eight hundred feet above the level of the sea, and is traversed by a winding road, very much like the passage over the Alps—the view gradually increased in beauty. At first we saw only the ridges of the rocky, wooded hills we had traversed during the day, on our journey from Atlanta. They were covered with oak, hickory, and chestnut trees, fields of majestic waving Indian corn and light graceful sugar-cane covering their base.

At the next turn of the road, which was overhung all the way with verdure, we came in sight of another range of mountains, the Blue Ridge chain. Beyond those, and seemingly higher in the clouds, the Alleghany formed, with the Cumberland Mountains on the other side, a mighty amphitheatre, some hundred miles in circumference, and on which the glowing rays of sunset then rested in deep crimson and purple hues.

Chattanooga town lay scattered about in the valley, looking like a child's toy village, the river Tennessee almost encircling it, and nearly forming an island, when it suddenly turns aside and hides itself from view, until it reappears in bright silvery curves about a mile further on. . . .

Winding up the steep, still higher and higher, we came right beneath a projecting cliff, which rose perpendicularly for several hundred feet, and on the top of which were some buildings. We looked up in amazement, and inquired if that was

"Mountain House," thinking that only eagles ever could reach it. But our horses, which were powerful ones, went straight on, only stopping now and then to take breath.

The grand panorama now unfolded itself in all its glory. From afar we had thought the higher chain of mountains reached the sky, but now, away, above, and beyond, a third faint outline was visible, seeming to mingle with the clouds; this was the Smoky Mountain range of North Carolina. As far as the eye could reach, these three chains of mountains formed an immense crescent, as though they encircled half the world. Surpassingly beautiful was the *coup d'oeil,* vying with anything we had seen in America. The foliage was resplendent in gold and crimson. Great eagles were sweeping through the glittering haze of the sunset, and so brilliantly *riante* was the splendour of the whole scene, that it was hard to believe, while gazing in rapture upon it, that strife, misery, and carnage had so lately been rife in that lovely valley. . . .

Indeed, after the hot, dusty, noisy pandemonium of Atlanta, with its 90 to 100 degrees of heat, and not a tree to shade one from the sun, or to rest the weary eyes upon, it seemed almost like ascending from purgatory to paradise.

YOSEMITE

One of the most stupendous marvels of the North American continent is the valley of the Yo Semite; attractive alike to the geologist, the naturalist, the artist, and the wonder-loving tourist; in a word, to mankind generally, both civilized and savage. So widely has its fame gone forth, that it has recently become quite the fashion to visit this grand workshop of nature, where she has been secretly labouring for thousands of years, unknown, unsuspected by what we are apt to consider the towering wisdom of man. . . .

For two days we rode, from early morning to dewy eve, through the most glorious country it has ever been my good fortune to traverse. Mountain rose above mountain, peak above peak; and away up, mingling with the snowy clouds, peered the no less snowy caps of the distant Sierra Nevada; and yet, looking down here and there, we could descry green valleys nestling among the mountains, and deep cañons filled with dark pines. . . .

It requires at least three weeks to visit the whole of these marvellous regions; for, besides the valley, there is a twin sister, called Hetch-Hetchy, with waterfalls averaging one thousand feet in height; also the little Yo Semite, called my valley, from the fact that I was the first white woman who ever scaled its rugged fastnesses; and I went through the necessary formula of planting my stick and throwing up my hat, which gives me a claim to several hundred acres of land. It is six thousand feet above the great Yo Semite, and seems like a reflection of it cast up in the sky. The river Mercede has its source in the mountains which encompass it. It winds through the upper valley, and rushes down to the lower one in two splendid waterfalls. . . .

Instead of three weeks which I had proposed to stay, I remained three months and traversed the country around. . . .

I had made up my mind to ride the whole hundred and fifty miles of my return journey to Mariposa on horseback, accompanied by an Indian, and doing as much as I could daily.

"My God!" said an English nobleman, who was then enjoying the pleasures of the happy land with me, "have you any idea to what you are exposing yourself? The Indians might murder you; the bears might devour you; you might be taken sick, and be unable to reach your destination for the night."

"Yes," returned I, "and the moon might fall and submerge us all in green cheese."

"Well," replied his lordship, "I do not see any courage in incurring unnecessary risk. We have with some difficulty got a carriage within fifty miles of this. Why will you not take a seat in it? We could all start together, and we will land you safely in Francisco." And so it was decided.

Fatalities are not to be met by any forethought. When the guide had gone off with the baggage-mule with all my wraps, and the lunch (the meal of the day), I found that I had more farewells to say than I had anticipated. I had been so happy, and so much cared for in the valley, that my departure became quite a mournful event, and I was fain to kiss some pet children over and over again, by way of getting rid of a surplus of feeling. My cavaliers rode about, impatiently regretful of every minute so consumed, for we had a long ride before us. When I did, finally, get mounted, I discovered I was on a bad saddle; so I said gaily to my escort—"Oh! pray ride on; we must change the saddle. I shall overtake you very shortly; pray go on."

As I knew every foot of the valley, and had often served *them* as guide, they obeyed me. I never did overtake them, never saw them again. They probably indulged in a gallop, which I did not, reserving my horse for the terrible ascent of ten thousand feet, and the fifty miles I had before me.

I started without any doubt as to meeting them at certain points. But I noticed that the heavens were beginning to be clouded, and a soughing wind whispered sadly of a storm at hand. Soon the rain began to fall. I urged my Rosinante on. Unfortunately he was as bad as the saddle, and I ought to have changed him too. But as I ascended the mountain the rain turned to hail, and then to snow. Thicker and thicker it fell, like leaves of the autumn trees when shaken by the west wind; deeper and deeper it lay, obscuring the pathway, and rendering the mountain-side one broken, jagged slope of rock, trees, and manganite bushes.

I remembered with anxiety that it was the period for the setting in of the snow-storm in these mountains. The snow falls to the depth of fifteen feet almost without stopping, and lies for six months in the year; so that the few inhabitants of the valley are shut in for that time.

My horse began to stumble and slip, missing the trail, which was now, like the rest of the scenery, concealed by a soft, white cushion. . . .

That livelong day we struggled, and stumbled, and fell, and rolled. I led him, and whipped him, and coaxed him to get him on. Sometimes the poor brute would come to a dead stand, putting out his fore feet and shaking his head dolefully, almost prophesying that we could never make that journey. By this time there was no sign left of the track by which we had ascended through the intricate rock and jungle, and I was sure we must be close to the spot where my friends were awaiting me. And there it was. I knew it again by the peculiar form of the cedars, whose singular arms grow without a slant, horizontally from the trunk. But no friends were there—not a sign of them; and I was six thousand feet up the mountain!

There was nothing for it but to push on and overtake them, or reach a small, dilapidated woodman's hut which I knew of, some eight miles away, where at least I might get shelter from the blinding fury of the elements. Little thought I that at the same hour my companions, and also the guide, were wandering desperate, lost, like myself, in another portion of the mountain. I knew that I must continue to ascend, and so I did. . . .

When the shadows of night fairly closed in, my situation was the desolation of despair. To continue was simply to invite a fall, and rush into the jaws of death. I remembered, in my agony, that I had noticed a hollow tree not very long ago. I got off my horse, led him back, groping my way, with the bridle over my arm, and providentially found my kind (though hollow) friend. I crept in, regardless of snakes, and drew the horse's head close to me, so as to profit by the warmth of his nostrils.

Having been wet through all day, and now beginning to freeze, I had to persevere in continued friction to keep up the circulation of the blood; and so the long watches of a dreary winter's night wore sadly away. . . . I longed—oh! how I longed—for daylight. And at last it came; and, with the aid of the tree which had so generously sheltered me, I mounted my poor beast, who, shaking and trembling in every limb, had evidently resigned himself to his fate, though I had made him eat a few leaves I had gathered from the overhanging boughs.

We crawled on for a few paces, not knowing whether to turn to the right or to the left. Snow mountains above us, snow precipices below us, snow in front of us, snow in the rear. Snow everywhere; nothing but snow between earth and heaven! I, in my blue riding-habit, being the only dark speck upon the great white expanse, when suddenly the sun came out—and oh! the glorious sight that burst upon me!

I forgot my hunger; I forgot my danger. I seemed to escape

for a moment from that spectre of death whose clammy shadow had enfolded me closer and closer during the vigils of the night.

Who amongst us has not felt something of rapturous exhilaration upon beholding the first fall of snow in the country? But here was a whole world of snow-clad beauty and grandeur. For miles and miles—yes, for fifty miles away—I could see dome after dome rise glistening up to heaven, as slanting bars of pink and amber coruscated on their sides like scintillations from morning angels' wings. . . .

I had to give up trying to ride, and led the horse by the bridle; and I had struggled for an hour or two with nothing worse than slips and bruises, when, on a sudden, I heard a sound—oh! joy it was!—the panting of a horse: and surely he must have a rider! We had been the last party in the Valley; but there might be some one leaving for the winter months. I raised my voice and shouted, "Help! help!" with all the wild delirium of rapture with which this sudden promise of rescue filled my soul.

My voice rent the air, clean and shrill; but there came no other answer than the echo of the mountains, which doled out "Help! help!" with a despairing wail. Again I heard the panting sound. It came from the other side of a high granite crag, around which there was but a very narrow ledge. I had to tempt it! The snow concealed its real dimensions; but I kept close in to the rock, testing well with my feet before I trod.

I rounded the corner with a beating heart and exultant hope, and found myself face to face with a —*grizzly bear*—so near that our eyes actually met; and I shall carry the memory of his expression to my dying day.

I do believe that beast saw the agony of my soul when this horrible crisis of my fate assailed me. He never attempted to touch me. He never moved the almost pitying eyes with which he regarded me.

I turned to fly—missed my footing—fell over the precipice— was caught for a moment by some Manzanita bushes growing to the rocks; then, bounding down, I struck upon cliff, and scaur, and bramble, and rock, now and again, until I lost consciousness. Of course it was the work of a second.

When I came to myself, the sun was high in heaven: I was lying in a deep ravine, the snow crimsoned with blood: and the fierce precipice looming ominously above me.

The Manzanita and the deep snow-bed had saved my life.

I had fallen into a ravine, through which in the early spring would roar a little mountain torrent.

I knew that if I had the strength to follow that track it would lead me in sight of the Valley. It might be ten or twenty miles; but there it went.

I rallied my strength for the effort, for I had lost my horse on the ledge where I had encountered the benevolent bear; and, without enumerating all the trials and difficulties I went through on the occasion, suffice it to say that I was found at the close of the second day, frozen and insensible, by a hunter; was carried to a shelter, and cared for with all that true Christian charity which we often find in the roughest natures. . . .

This was the end of my visit to the Great Yo-Semite.

Maria Theresa Longworth, an Irishwoman, was educated in a French convent, and after the Crimean war she joined the French Sisters of Mercy in nursing the sick at the hospital of Galata. Major Yelverton had served with the Royal Army in Crimea.

While in Yosemite she contributed two articles based on her memories of the Sisters of Mercy to the Overland Monthly. *The same magazine contained an article in its November 1871 issue by Mary Viola Lawrence about the Countess and her snow terror. She says Maria Theresa was rescued by Mr. Leidig, who took her to Hutchings' Hotel. The bear was "a cinnamon bear."*

The Countess's sojourn became part of the Yosemite story. In 1871 her melodramatic novel, Zanita, A Tale of the Yosemite, *was published. Characters in the novel are based on real persons she met in the Valley, including John Muir, Charles Warren Stoddard, and members of the Hutchings family. The dates of her birth and death are variously reported, as were the "facts" of her life, for she embellished her own story with fanciful details. According to the* Complete Peerage, *under "Avonmore," she died in South Africa in 1881.*

Maria Theresa Longworth, *1870's*

Maria Theresa Longworth, Teresina in America. *New York: Arno Press, 1974. Vol. I, viii, 224-27, 229; II, 58, 67, 80—90. This is a reprint of* Teresina in America, *by* Thérèse Yelverton (Viscountess Avonmore). *London: Richard Bentley, 1875.*

16

Marianne North's American Landscapes

Marianne North (1830–1890) was an English botanical explorer. She traveled extensively in Europe with her father, and after his death in 1869 she ventured alone on the first of numerous trips that would take her to many exotic places in the world.

1871

I had long had the dream of going to some tropical country to paint its peculiar vegetation on the spot in natural abundant luxuriance; so when my friend Mrs. S. asked me to come and spend the summer with her in the United States, I thought this might easily be made into a first step for carrying out my plan, as average people in England have but a very confused idea of the difference between North and South America.

MASSACHUSETTS

I paid a visit to Mr. and Mrs. [Charles Francis] Adams at Quincy, one of the oldest houses in America, full of curious family portraits and furniture, large low rooms, big open fireplaces, many windows, and old brocade hangings. Except for the outside being entirely of wood, it might have been taken for a two hundred years old manor house in England.

Mr. A. had lately added a stone fireproof library, detached, in the garden, to keep all his precious books and manuscripts in, for he had whole volumes of Washington's letters, and many besides written by all his greatest countrymen. His father and grandfather had both been Presidents; he might have been one himself, but he never would allow himself to be put forward as a political candidate at home, though he was long his country's representative in England. He was a remarkably quiet man, but his good wife made up for it, and her genial chatter used to make him sit and shake with laughter. It was a very pleasant family to be in, all the sons and his daughter had such a thorough respect for their parents, and when he did speak he was always worth listening to.

The two elder sons had built houses within ten minutes' walk of their father's, and came in every morning to have a talk with him, going into Boston in the morning to their business and back by rail. Their children and wives were in and out all day long.

From Colonel A.'s house there was a glorious view over sea and land, the former being about a mile off, and the whole coast broken up by estuaries, islands, and points connected by low isthmuses, so that one could never feel quite sure where the sea began and the land ended, being in that respect much like the island of Rügen [Germany].

The floors, staircases, and chimney-pieces were of different sorts of wood—black walnut, butternut, hickory, ash, and pine—beautifully put together, with very little ornament, sometimes a line or simple geometrical pattern cut and filled with blue or red, and the rich natural colour of the wood kept as a ground-work. Though the house was on top of a hill there was abundant water everywhere. In the old house at Quincy was one room wainscoted with polished mahogany.

The C. F.s [i.e., James T. Fields] were spending the summer near us at West Manchester, and were very good to me when Mrs. S. was away. He was partner of Ticknor, and editor of the *Atlantic Monthly*, and she a pretty poetess who went into floods of tears at the mere mention of Charles Dickens, whose name resembled that of his own "Mrs. 'Arris" in their mouths, and their room was hung all around with portraits of their hero.

I enjoyed my expeditions with him and his wife. He invited me to meet Mrs. [Louis] Agassiz at a picnic one day, and called for me in his pony carriage, picked her up at the railway station, and drove us to one of the many beautiful high headlands on the coast; then we walked over the cliffs to find a most curious old cedar-tree, perfectly shaved at the top like an umbrella pine by the sea winds, with its branches matted and twisted in the most fantastical way underneath, and clinging to the very edge of the precipice, its roots being tightly wedged into a crack without any apparent earth to nourish it. It was said to be of unknown antiquity, and there was no other specimen of such a cedar in the country; it looked to me like the common sort we call red cedar. We sat and talked a long while under its shade.

Mrs. Agassiz and I agreed that the greatest pleasure we knew was to see new and wonderful countries, and the only rival to that pleasure was the one of staying quietly at home. Only ignorant fools think because one likes sugar one cannot like salt; those people are only capable of one idea, and never try experiments.

Mrs. A. was a most agreeable handsome woman; she had begun life as a rich, ball-going young lady, then, on her father losing his fortune, she had started a girls' school to support her family [Harvard Annex, now Radcliffe], and finally married the clever old Swiss professor, whose children were already settled in the world. She made an excellent stepmother as well as travelling companion, putting his voyages and lectures together in such a manner that the Americans had a riddle, "Why were *Agassiz's Travels* like a mermaiden?" "Because you could not tell where the woman ended and the fish began!"

The Professor was a great pet of the Americans, who were then just fitting up a new exploring ship for him to go on a ten months' voyage to Cape Horn and the Straits of Magellan to hunt for prehistoric fish in comfort. She told me much of the wonders and delights of her famous Amazon expedition, and promised me letters there if I went.

After a delightful morning we drove on to the woods behind

Mr. F.'s house, and found luncheon spread for us, Mrs. T. and her sister, in white aprons and caps, acting servant-maids and waiting on us. Mr. F. let off a perfect cascade of anecdotes, and then I was taken into the house to do my part of the entertainment and sing for an hour, which I grudged much, as I preferred listening; but I suppose they liked it, as one of the ladies wept bitterly. After this we had tea on the piazza, and looked down on the great wild cliffs and deep blue sea a thousand feet below us.

Another day I went by street-car from Boston to Cambridge, and met two pretty girls, who spoke to me and told me they were the Miss Longfellows. When we got to the end of the journey, their father came and took me for a walk round the different Colleges, and home to have lunch with him in the house Washington used to live in. It was quite in what we English call the Queen Anne style, with plenty of fine trees round it, and large wainscoted rooms full of pictures and pretty things. The luncheon was worthy of a poet—nothing but cakes and fruit, and cold tea with lumps of ice in it; he was a model poet to listen to and look at, with his snow-white hair, eager eyes, and soft gentle manner and voice, full of pleasant unpractical talk, quite too good for everyday use. He showed me all his treasures, and asked me to come and stay with them if I returned to Boston, after which he showed me the way to Mrs. A[gassiz]'s house.

I found her and the Professor even more to my mind; he spoke funny broken English, and looked entirely content with himself and everybody else. They showed me photographs and told me of all the wonders of Brazil, and what I was to do there, then gave me a less poetical dinner. Then Mrs. Agassiz took me to the Museum and made Count Pourtalez take us up to the attic to see the most perfect collection of palms in the world (all mummies), intensely interesting, as illustrating the world's history. Mrs. Agassiz showed me the great sheath of one of the flowers, which native mothers use as a cradle and also as a baby's bath, it being quite water-tight. The flowers of some of the palms were two to three yards long. She said, though she had wandered whole days in the forests, she had never seen a snake nor a savage beast. One day she heard a great crashing through the tangle and felt rather frightened, when a harmless milk-cow came out.

After seeing the palms she caught a German professor and made him show us a most splendid collection of gorgeous butterflies: I never saw any so beautiful; they were all locked up in dark drawers, as the light faded them. Then came corals and madrepores.

I missed my train . . .

WASHINGTON

I had a card brought me . . . "the Secretary of State" and Mr. [Hamilton] Fish followed it, to whom I had a letter of introduction. He was a great massive man, with a hard sensible head. He said he would call for me in the evening, and take me to the White House. So at eight o'clock in he came again after another big card, I being all ready for him in bonnet and shawl, and in no small trepidation at having to talk *tête-à-tête* with the Prime Minister in a small brougham. However, I found there was no need, as he did it all himself.

We were shown in first to the awful crimson satin room which Mrs. G[urney] had described to me, with a huge picture of the Grant family all standing side by side for their portraits. Then we were told to come upstairs, and passed from state-rooms to ordinary everyday life up a back staircase, which was the only means of reaching the upper storey allowed by the architect of seventy years ago. We were shown into a comfortable library and living-room, where a very old man sat reading the newspaper, Mrs. Grant's papa, who did not understand or hear any of the remarks Mr. Fish or I made to him. Then came Mrs. Grant, a motherly, kind body; then at last came the President, also a most homely kind of man.

We at first sat rather wide apart, and I had more of the talk to do than I enjoyed, and felt like a criminal being examined till Mrs. Grant hunted up a German book full of dried grasses to show me, and the poor withered sticks and straws brought dear Nature back again. I put on my spectacles and knelt down at Mrs. Grant's knee to look at them. They began to find out I was not a fine-lady worshipper of Worth, and we all got chatty and happy. Mrs. Grant confessed she had no idea "Governor Fish had brought me with him, or she would not have let me upstairs, but didn't mind now"; and she told me all about her children; and if I stayed long enough would, I have no doubt, have confided to me her difficulties about servants also. . . .

The next morning I found a big envelope with a huge G. on it, and a card inside from the President and Mrs. Grant asking me to dinner that night. The [Russell] Gurneys had another, so we went in state and were shown into the blue satin oval room, well adapted for that sort of ceremony, and the aide-de-camp General Porter came and made himself most agreeable to us. Then came two Senators and the Secretary of Foreign Affairs, and then the President and his wife arm in arm, with Miss Nelly and a small brother, and grandpapa toddling in after. He had an armchair given to him, and General Grant told me he was so heavy that he had broken half the chairs in the house, and they were very careful about giving him extra strong ones now.

After a terrible five minutes, dinner was announced, and to my horror the President offered me his arm and walked me in first (greatness thrust upon me). I looked penitently across at Mrs. Gurney, who looked highly amused at my confusion, and did not pity me in the least. I was relieved by finding the great man did not care to talk while he ate, and General Porter was easy to get on with on my other side. He seemed to know every place, inhabited and uninhabited, in America. . . .

The G[urney]s were quite surprised (as I was) at the fuss the Grants had made about me, as they never gave dinners (they themselves had only dined there once before, when the High Commissioners first went over). I could not think what I had done to deserve all this; but after I left it came out. Mrs. Grant talked of me as the daughter of Lord North, the ex-Prime Minister of England. I always knew I was old, but was not prepared for that amount of antiquity.

Miss North spent the rest of 1871 and 1872 in Jamaica, and, after a short visit to her London home, she set off for Brazil. This trip was followed by another to Japan in 1875, via the United States. When she reached the Pacific coast she visited the Big Trees and Yosemite.

1875

I got an old miner "guard" and a horse, left Clarks at six for the "Big Trees" of the Mariposa Grove, and had a long day's work among them.

The whole road was beautiful, through the biggest trees of the fir kind I ever saw, till I saw "The Trees." All the world now knows their dimensions, so I need not repeat them; but only those who have seen them know their rich red plush bark and the light green eclipse of feathery foliage above, and the giant trunks which swell enormously at the base, having no branches up to a third of their whole height. . . . There were about seven hundred in that one grove of Mariposa alone, and three other groves within a day or two of them. They stood out grandly against the other trees, which in themselves would be worth a journey to see—sugar-pines, yellow-pines, and *arbor vitae*, hung with golden lichen.

The forest was full of strange trails of big bears and other wild animals. I was told that the bear-steps were probably those of "old Joe," who had been known "just about there" for the last twenty years, and was a kind of Mrs. 'Arris to travellers. I was shown many of those funny little perforated larders the woodpeckers made for the squirrels to put their nuts in.

The descent into the Yosemite gave perhaps the very best general view of the valley; so I got our driver, after he had rested his horses and dined, to give me a lift up the hill again as far as that view, and leave me to paint it. He told Colonel and Mrs. M., who were going on with him, that "I was one of the right sort. I neither cared for bears nor yet for Ingins," and he absolutely refused to take a dollar from me when I offered it.

But I had only two or three hours before dark. I could do nothing satisfactorily. The view was "very big," but to my taste that was its chief merit. It was like a magnified Swiss valley, the gray granite cliffs looking as hard and inharmonious as Dolomites; they were shaped like them or like the Organ Mountains of Brazil, and even their great height (3000 feet of sheer precipice) was dwarfed by the enormous size of the pines on and about them.

MARIPOSA GROVE

I had a long day's work in that lovely forest, painting the huge tree called the Great Grisly, whose first side branch is as big as any trunk in Europe. . . . After that I went down to 'Frisco and became No. 794 in the Occidental Hotel.

North's careful botanical paintings are now in the North Gallery, which she donated to the Royal Botanic Garden at Kew, England. In the gallery she placed a dado of 246 panels of woods collected from all over the world. Perhaps she was inspired by the Adams house in Quincy.

She traveled continuously from 1871 until 1882, visiting almost every continent and numerous islands in the Pacific and the Atlantic. In 1881, returning from New Zealand, she crossed the United States again, visiting more big trees and Yosemite and, in the East, the lush gardens of Staten Island. In her travels she discovered many new plants, some of which were named for her.

Recollections of a Happy Life: Being the Autobiography of Marianne North, *ed. Mrs. John Addington Symonds. London and New York: Macmillan, 1892. Vol. I, 39, 46–50, 73–76, 202–3, 204. A shortened version of her recollections, with beautiful color reproductions of some of her paintings, was published in collaboration with the Royal Botanic Gardens, Kew, as* A Vision of Eden: The Life and Work of Marianne North. *New York: Holt, Rinehart and Winston, 1980.*

17

Emily Faithfull on the "Redundant Woman"

Emily Faithfull (1835–1895) made three visits to the United States between 1872 and 1884 to see "how America is trying to solve the most delicate and difficult problem presented by modern civilization"—the problem of women's employment. She had established, in 1860, the Victoria Press in London, where she trained and employed women compositors. In 1862 she was appointed Printer and Publisher in Ordinary to Her Majesty. At the time of her first visit to America she was recognized as a leading promoter of women's employment in England.

She said that the most memorable event of her visit was a reception given her at Steinway Hall in New York City on January 29, 1873.

The programme of the Reception Committee is a record of the representative ladies of New York, all eminent in literature, art, science, and industry. . . . Mrs. Henry Field, who occupied the chair, gave me a formal and generous welcome, and then spoke at length on the dignity of labor, claiming that the woman who supports herself is entitled to ascend in the social as she does in the moral scale; not to be pitied or patronized, but to be respected for her spirit of independence. . . .

Mrs. Field made an eloquent appeal to all present "to avoid an idle, aimless life, dependence upon friends, or, what is worse, marriage to escape work or to gain a position. . . . With women rests the power to right their sex from an absurd prejudice."

I just missed the meetings of the State Agricultural College at Denver, at which Mrs. Olive Wright read a very interesting paper on "What women are doing in Colorado." Some women seem to be mining; the first prize at the last State fair was taken by a lady for skillful horsemanship and horse-breaking; and much of the value of the domestic cattle industry is, according to her paper, due to them.

I certainly heard of girls on the prairies, who seemed to like a tramp over the plains in search of the boundary line of her father's "claim" as much as the daughter of a British sportsman enjoys a morning on a Scotch moor during the grouse-shooting season. They become as used to handling the rifle as the plough, and many of the pioneer ladies I heard of were pursuing their studies in their prairie homes. Some have gone through trials which even would shake the nerves of the sterner sex. I was told of a widow who had built her own "claim shack," had it twice blown away by tornadoes and once burned to the ground in the course of two years; but she holds on to the life she has chosen, and in face and form is the embodiment of health.

1884

When Harriet Martineau visited America in 1840, she found only seven occupations open to women; today, in Massachusetts alone, there are nearly three hundred different branches of industry by which women can earn from one hundred to three thousand dollars a year. The ten years even which elapsed between my first tour in 1872 and my second in 1882, had brought about marked changes. The type-writer at the first date was in its tenderest infancy, and the telephone was un-known; now both these marvellous inventions are giving hundreds of girls throughout the States remunerative work, and many artistic occupations have also been developed.

It is indeed cheerful to record these improvements, but still it must not be supposed that American ladies can find employment whenever they need it. I received many letters from strangers, as well as from persons well-known to me, which proved conclusively that there are still great difficulties to be encountered by those who are obliged to earn their own livelihood.

A heartless hoax, practiced on a New York firm in the early part of 1883, clearly showed that many are vainly searching for work in that city. An advertisement appeared in the *Herald*, stating that four lady copyists were required by a Wall Street firm, for ten dollars each per week. The next day the office was simply besieged by eager applicants, many of whom had spent car fares they could ill afford, only to find that a fruitless journey, entailing a bitter disappointment, was due to a stupid joke on the firm itself.

In 1872 I was hospitably entertained by a lady whose husband was a General in the United States army. I found her in 1883 struggling for the means whereby to live, as his death and other misfortunes had left her penniless.

This spring a Brooklyn gentleman advertised for a lady copyist at a salary of seven dollars a week, and his wife for a cook at ten. There was only one applicant for the cook's place, while 456 ladies were anxious to secure the post of copyist.

Such facts have induced some people, in both countries, to point to domestic service as affording the needed opening for "redundant women." . . . I can not admit that domestic service is a reasonable channel for the employment of educated ladies, although I consider that no honest work is as derogatory as idleness. . . . Who would not smile if the proposition were advanced of clergymen's and physicians' sons going out as valets, footmen, and butlers? Classes and sexes must sink or swim together; that which is impossible for the man can not be made available—speaking from the class point of view—for the woman.

"A Woman Switchman" certainly sounds extraordinary, but one who appears quite contented with her lot has been employed in that way for many years at the railroad junction at

Macon, Ga., and has never been known to misplace a switch. When asked how she liked the work, which occupies her from 6 a.m. to 6 at night, she replied, "Far better than the wash-tub. I am never sick, and I know when my work is done."

Perhaps there is a general dislike to "the wash-tub" in America; anyhow the heads of the laundries are invariably men, and a great deal of money is made, as machinery is far more generally used than in England, but which, with the preparations used in washing, often play sad havoc with the clothes.

A steamboat captain seems an equally singular employment for a woman to adopt, but Mrs. Mary S. Miller has received a license from the New Orleans Board of United States Inspectors of Steam Vessels to run the Mississippi steamboat *Saline*, together with permission to navigate on the Red, Ouachita, and other Western rivers. She holds that a woman can manage a boat as well as a sewing-machine, and having passed her examination and proved her capacity, the inspectors were bound to grant her certificate, for they had submitted Mrs. Miller's application to the Secretary of the Navy, being at a loss to know what to do in such an unprecedented case. That office gallantly replied, "If she demonstrated her competence for the position the license was to be granted." Mrs. Miller is accordingly now in full exercise of a calling which demands exceptional energy, nerve, and discretion. . . .

Mrs. Maxwell, of Colorado, struck out in a novel direction; by her own personal efforts she collected a vast number of birds and animals, which she shot, and afterward skinned and stuffed for sale. Bears, antelopes, and elks from the Rocky Mountains, prairie dogs, squirrels and beavers which fell a prey to her gun, and all sorts of birds, have been thus utilized for business purposes.

Mrs. Maxwell's pursuit will probably be condemned by some people as "most unfeminine" . . .

Many women are employed throughout the States as book agents. The manager of Messrs. Houghton, Mifflin & Co. told me of a school-teacher who had adopted this mode of living, and started out to obtain subscribers for the "American Encyclopaedia." She has never netted less than five thousand dollars a year, and only works for eight or nine months, and travels in a carriage from door to door with introductions from previous customers.

In England, Emily continued her efforts to create opportunities for women. In 1886 her work was recognized by a gift of £100 from the Royal Bounty; from 1889 until her death six years later she received a Civil List Pension.

Emily Faithfull, Three Visits to America. *New York: Fowler and Wells, 1884. Pages 14–17, 137–38, 292–95, 217–20.*

18

Isabella Bird Makes Herself Agreeable

Isabella Bird (1831–1904), whose first visit to the United States was in 1854 (see pages 91–97), returned in 1873, much improved in health and vitality after a long trip to the Sandwich Islands. She spent the summer and autumn in the West. Her goal was Estes Park, Colorado. She had made her way as far as Fort Collins, hoping to get a horse she could ride through the mountains. She accepted a ride in a buggy to a place where, she had been told, there was a boarding-house and where she supposed she could stay until a horse, or at least a guide, could be found to put her on her way.

CANYON, COLORADO, SEPTEMBER 12, 1873

The solitude was becoming somber, when, after driving for nine hours, and traveling at the least forty-five miles, without any sign of fatigue on the part of the *broncos*, we came to a stream, by the side of which we drove along a definite track, till we came to a sort of tri-partite valley, with a majestic crooked canyon 2,000 feet deep opening upon it. A rushing stream roared through it, and the Rocky Mountains, with pines scattered over them, came down upon it.

A little farther, and the canyon became utterly inaccessible. This was exciting; here was an inner world. A rough and shaky bridge, made of the outsides of pines laid upon some unsecured logs, crossed the river. The *broncos* stopped and smelt it,

125

not liking it, but some encouraging speech induced them to go over. On the other side was a log cabin, partially ruinous, and the very rudest I ever saw, its roof of plastered mud being broken into large holes. It stood close to the water among some cotton-wood trees. A little higher there was a very primitive saw-mill, also out of repair, with some logs lying about. An emigrant wagon and a forlorn tent, with a camp-fire and a pot, were in the foreground, but there was no trace of the boarding-house, of which I stood a little in dread.

The driver went for further directions to the log cabin, and returned with a grim smile deepening the melancholy of his face to say it was Mr. Chalmers', but there was no accommodation for such as him, much less for me! This was truly "a sell." I got down and found a single room of the rudest kind, with the wall at one end partially broken down, and no furniture but two chairs and two unplaned wooden shelves, with some sacks of straw upon them for beds. There was an adjacent cabin room, with a stove, benches, and table, where they cooked and ate, but this was all.

A hard, sad-looking woman looked at me measuringly. She said that they sold milk and butter to parties who camped in the canyon, that they had never had any boarders but two asthmatic old ladies, but they would take me for five dollars per week if I "would make myself agreeable."

The horses had to be fed, and I sat down on a box, had some dried beef and milk, and considered the matter. If I went back to Fort Collins, I thought I was farther from a mountain life, and had no choice but Denver, a place from which I shrank, or to take the cars for New York. Here the life was rough, rougher than any I had ever seen, and the people repelled me by their faces and manners; but if I could rough it for a few days, I might, I thought, get over canyons and all other difficulties into Estes Park, which has become the goal of my journey and hopes. So I decided to remain.

SEPTEMBER 16

Five days here, and I am no nearer Estes Park. How the days pass I know not; I am weary of the limitations of this existence. This is "a life in which nothing happens."

When the buggy disappeared, I felt as if I had cut the bridge behind me. I sat down and knitted for some time—my usual resource under discouraging circumstances. I really did not know how I should get on. There was no table, no bed, no basin, no towel, no glass, no window, no fastening on the door. The roof was in holes, the logs were unchinked, and one end of the cabin was partially removed! Life was reduced to its simplest elements.

I went out; the family all had something to do, and took no notice of me. I went back, and then an awkward girl of sixteen, with uncombed hair, and a painful repulsiveness of face and air, sat on a log for half an hour and stared at me. I tried to draw her into talk, but she twirled her fingers and replied snappishly in monosyllables. Could I by any effort "make myself agreeable"? I wondered.

The day went on. I put on my Hawaiian dress, rolling up the sleeves to the elbows in an "agreeable" fashion. Towards evening the family returned to feed, and pushed some dried beef and milk in at the door. They all slept under the trees, and before dark carried the sacks of straw out for their bedding. I followed their example that night, or rather watched Charles's Wain [the Big Dipper] while they slept, but since then have slept on blankets on the floor under the roof.

They have neither lamp nor candle, so if I want to do anything after dark I have to do it by the unsteady light of pine knots. As the nights are cold, and free from bugs, and I do a good deal of manual labor, I sleep well. At dusk I make my bed on the floor, and draw a bucket of ice-cold water from the river; the family go to sleep under the trees, and I pile logs on the fire sufficient to burn half the night, for I assure you the solitude is *eerie* enough.

There are unaccountable noises, (wolves), rummagings under the floor, queer cries, and stealthy sounds of I know not what. One night a beast (fox or skunk) rushed in at the open end of the cabin, and fled through the window, almost brushing my face, and on another, the head and three or four inches of the body of a snake were protruded through a chink of the floor close to me, to my extreme disgust. My mirror is the polished inside of my watchcase.

At sunrise Mrs. Chalmers comes in—if coming into a nearly open shed can be called *in*—and makes a fire, because she thinks me too stupid to do it, and mine is the family room; and by seven I am dressed, have folded the blankets, and swept the floor, and then she puts some milk and bread or stirabout [porridge] on a box by the door. After breakfast I draw more water, and wash one or two garments daily, taking care that there are no witnesses of my inexperience. Yesterday a calf sucked one into hopeless rags.

The rest of the day I spend in mending, knitting, writing to you, and the various odds and ends which arise when one has to do all for oneself. At twelve and six some food is put on the box by the door, and at dusk we make up our beds.

A distressed emigrant woman has just given birth to a child in a temporary shanty by the river, and I go to help her each day. I have made the acquaintance of all the careworn, struggling settlers within a walk. All have come for health, and most have found or are finding it, even if they have not better shelter than a wagon tilt or a blanket on sticks laid across four poles. The climate of Colorado is considered the finest in North America, and consumptives, asthmatics, dyspeptics, and sufferers from nervous diseases, are here in hundreds and thousands, either trying the "camp cure" for three or four months, or settling here permanently. . . .

I am forming a plan for getting farther into the mountains, and hope that my next letter will be more lively.

CANYON, SEPTEMBER

The absence of a date shows my predicament. *They* have no newspaper; *I* have no almanack; the father is away for the day, and none of the others can help me, and they look contemptuously upon my desire for information on the subject. The monotony will come to an end to-morrow, for Chalmers offers to be my guide over the mountains to Estes Park, and has persuaded his wife "for once to go for a frolic"; and with much reluctance, many growls at the waste of time, and many apprehensions of danger and loss, she has consented to accompany him.

My life has grown less dull from their having become more interesting to me, and as I have "made myself agreeable," we are on fairly friendly terms. My first move in the direction of fraternizing was, however, snubbed. A few days ago, having finished my own work, I offered to wash up the plates, but Mrs. C., with a look which conveyed more than words, a curl of her nose, and a sneer in her twang, said "Guess you'll make more work nor you'll do. Those hands of yours" (very brown and coarse they were) "ain't no good; never done nothing, I guess. . . ."

Since then I have risen in their estimation by improvizing a lamp—Hawaiian fashion—by putting a wisp of rag into a tin of fat. They have actually condescended to sit up till the stars come out since. Another advance was made by means of the shell-pattern quilt I am knitting for you. There has been a tendency toward approving of it, and a few days since the girl snatched it out of my hand, saying, "I want this," and apparently took it to the camp. This has resulted in my having a knitting class, with the woman, her married daughter, and a woman from the camp, as pupils. Then I have gained ground with the man by being able to catch and saddle a horse. . . .

But oh! what a hard, narrow life it is with which I am now in contact! A narrow and unattractive religion, which I believe still to be genuine, and an intense but narrow patriotism, are the only higher influences. Chalmers came from Illinois nine years ago, pronounced by the doctors to be far gone in consumption, and in two years he was strong. They are a queer family; somewhere in the remote Highlands I have seen such another. Its head is tall, gaunt, lean, and ragged, and has lost one eye. On an English road one would think him a starving or a dangerous beggar.

He is slightly intelligent, very opinionated, and wishes to be thought well informed, which he is not. . . . He considers himself a profound theologian, and by the pine logs at night discourses to me on the mysteries of the eternal counsels and the divine decrees. . . . He hates England with a bitter, personal hatred. . . . He is very fond of talking, and asks me a great deal about my travels, but if I speak favorably of the climate or resources of any other country, he regards it as a slur on Colorado. . . . Yet Chalmers is a frugal, sober, hard-working man, and he, his eldest son, and a "hired man" "Rise early," "going forth to their work and labor till the evening;" and if they do not "late take rest," they truly "eat the bread of carefulness." It is hardly surprising that nine years of persevering shiftlessness should have resulted in nothing but the ability to procure the bare necessaries of life.

Of Mrs. C. I can say less. She looks like one of the English poor women of our childhood—lean, clean, toothless, and speaks, like some of them, in a piping, discontented voice, which seems to convey a personal reproach. All her waking hours are spent in a large sun-bonnet. She is never idle for one minute, is severe and hard, and despises everything but work. I think she suffers from her husband's shiftlessness. She always speaks of me as "This" or "that woman." . . .

You will now have some idea of my surroundings. It is a moral, hard, unloving, unlovely, unrelieved, unbeautified, grinding life. These people live in a discomfort and lack of ease and refinements which seems only possible to people of British stock. . . .

An English physician is settled about half a mile from here over a hill. He is spoken of as holding "very extreme opinions." Chalmers rails at him for being "a thick-skulled Englishman," for being "fine, polished," etc. To say a man is "polished" here is to give him a very bad name. He accuses him also of holding views subversive of all morality.

In spite of all this, I thought he might possess a map, and I induced Mrs. C. to walk over with me. She intended it as a formal morning call, but she wore the inevitable sun-bonnet, and had her dress tied up as when washing. It was not till I reached the gate that I remembered that I was in my Hawaiian riding dress, and that I still wore the spurs with which I had been trying a horse in the morning!

The house was in a grass valley which opened from the

tremendous canyon through which the river had cut its way. The Foot Hills, with their terraces of flaming red rock, were glowing in the sunset, and a pure green sky arched tenderly over a soft evening scene. Used to the meanness and baldness of settlers' dwellings, I was delighted to see that in this instance the usual log cabin was only the lower floor of a small house, which bore a delightful resemblance to a Swiss châlet. It stood in a vegetable garden fertilized by an irrigating ditch, outside of which were a barn and cowshed.

A young Swiss girl was bringing the cows slowly home from the hill, an Englishwoman in a clean print dress stood by the fence holding a baby, and a fine-looking Englishman in a striped Garibaldi shirt, and trousers of the same tucked into high boots, was shelling corn.

As soon as Mrs. Hughes spoke I felt she was truly a lady; and oh! how refreshing her refined, courteous, graceful English manner was, as she invited us into the house! The entrance was low, through a log porch festooned and almost concealed by a "wild cucumber." Inside, though plain and poor, the room looked a home, not like a squatter's cabin. An old tin was completely covered by a graceful clematis . . . and white muslin curtains, and above all two shelves of admirably-chosen books, gave the room almost the air of elegance. Why do ·I write almost? It was an oasis. It was barely three weeks since I had left "the communion of educated men," and the first tones of the voices of my host and hostess made me feel as if I had been out of it for a year.

Mrs. C. stayed an hour and a half, and then went home to the cows, when we launched upon a sea of congenial talk. They said they had not seen an educated lady for two years, and pressed me to go and visit them. I rode home on Dr. Hughes's horse after dark, to find neither fire nor light in the cabin. Mrs. C. had gone back saying, "Those English talked just like savages, I couldn't understand a word they said."

I made a fire, and extemporized a light with some fat and a wick of rag, and Chalmers came in to discuss my visit and to ask me a question concerning a matter which had roused the latent curiosity of the whole family. I had told him, he said, that I knew no one hereabouts, but "his woman" told him that Dr. H. and I spoke constantly of a Mrs. Grundy, whom we both knew and disliked, and who was settled, as we said, not far off! He had never heard of her, he said, and he was the pioneer settler of the canyon, and there was a man up here from Longmount who said he was sure there was not a Mrs. Grundy in the district, unless it was a woman who went by two names!

The wife and family had then come in, and I felt completely nonplussed. I longed to tell Chalmers that it was he and such as he, there or anywhere, with narrow hearts, bitter tongues, and harsh judgments, who were the true "Mrs. Grundys," dwarfing individuality, checking lawful freedom of speech, and making men "offenders for a word," but I forbore. How I extricated myself from the difficulty, deponent sayeth not.

After more adventures in the mountains, Isabella finally reached Estes Park and "grandeur, cheerfulness, health, enjoyment, novelty, freedom, etc. etc." She spent the winter there, met another Englishman who enchanted her (though he was a rough, one-eyed, self-confessed murderer), and climbed Long's Peak (hauled up by the Englishman).

Bird's travels took her into many different countries, and her books made her, in her day, the most famous of Victorian travel writers. The sister Henrietta, to whom she had written her letters, died in 1880, and at the age of fifty Isabella married Dr. Bishop, the physician who had attended Henrietta. During the five years of her marriage she did not travel, but after the doctor died she resumed her journeying. Her later books were published under the name of Isabella Bishop.

Isabella L. Bird, A Lady's Life in the Rocky Mountains. *Norman, Oklahoma: University of Oklahoma Press, 1960. Pages 38–47, 50–53. First published in London: Murray, 1879.*

19

Helena Modjeska in the Golden West

Madam Helena Modjeska (1840–1909) was for some years the leading actress at the Imperial Theater in Warsaw. She was married to Karol Bozenta Chlapowski. In 1875 she was in ill health, brought on, she believed, by the political condition, "where government persecution penetrates into the most intimate recesses of private life." The following light-hearted conversation took place in the couple's living room.

WARSAW, POLAND, WINTER 1875

Someone brought news of the coming Centennial Exposition in America. [Henry] Sienkiewicz, with his vivid imagination, described the unknown country in the most attractive terms. Maps were brought out and California discussed. It was worth while to hear the young men's various opinions about the Golden West:—

"You cannot die of hunger there, that is quite sure!" said one. "Rabbits, hares, and partridges are unguarded! You have only to go out and shoot them!"

"Yes," said another, "and fruits, too, are plenty! Blackberries and the fruit of the cactus grow wild, and they say the latter is simply delicious!"

"I have heard," said another, "that the fruit of California is at least three times larger than in any other country!"

"Yes, everything is extraordinary!" sounded the reply.

133

"Fancy, coffee grows wild there! All you have to do is to pick it; also pepper and the castor-oil bean, and ever so many useful plants! One could make an industry of it!"

"Besides gold!" said a wise voice. "Gold! They say you can dig it out almost anywhere!"

"There are also rattlesnakes," added [Victor] Baranski, in a cynical tone of voice.

"Yes! But who cares! You can kill them with a stick!"

"Oh, how brave you are,—sitting in this cosy room!" said our sceptical friend.

"Rattlesnakes are bad, of course, but think of a grizzly bear and a puma, the California jaguar!"

"What a glorious hunt one could have!" exclaimed Sienkiewicz, and then added, "I should like to go and see that country of sunshine and primitive nature!"

Everyone had to say something about the promised land, and [Stanley] Witkiewicz took a pencil and drew fantastic pictures of my nieces sitting on two huge mushrooms, while an enormous rattlesnake was nestling at their feet. The cherries that hung on branches over their heads were as large as apples. Dr. Karwowski entered just when we were most interested in Sienkiewicz's description of an imaginary storm on the ocean, and said to me jokingly:—

"You need a change of air, Madame. Why not make a trip to America?"

"That is a good idea," my husband answered. "Why not?" and he looked at me.

I repeated, smiling, "Why not?"

[Adam] Chmielowski laughed and exclaimed: "Let us all go. We will kill pumas, build huts, make our own garments out of skins, and live as our forefathers lived!"

"Just so!" added Baranski. "And Pani [Mother] Helena will cook and wash dishes, and instead of violets and heliotrope, her perfume will be the flavor of dishwater. How enticing!" We all laughed, and the subject was dismissed as an impossibility.
. . . Then one morning during the Christmas holidays my son Rudolphe, whom I had sent to Cracow with my mother in order to place him in a Polish school, came to Warsaw to spend

his short vacation with us. He was even then determined to become a civil engineer. The first thing he spoke of was the coming exposition in America; and the lad, looking at the maps, declared that some day he would build the Panama Canal. He said it would be so nice if we could go to America now, see the great fair, and then cross Panama to California. He looked so happy planning his journey, that both my husband and myself began to look upon the crossing of the ocean as a possibility. "Why not?" we repeated again, and my son put his arms around our necks and kissing us in turn, said, "Oh, let us go there soon."

The impossible became a reality in July, 1876. Madame Modjeska, Chlapowski (later called Count Bozenta by the Americans), and Rudolph, set off for America. Along with them went Jules Sypniewski, his wife and two little children, Lucian Paprocki, and a sixteen-year-old nursemaid, fresh out of a convent. Sienkiewicz and Sypniewski had already visited the New World and gave glowing accounts of California. Chlapowski, a Polish aristocrat who had spent a year in a Prussian prison for revolutionary activities, envisioned the establishment of a colony on the model of New England's Brook Farm.

They reached Anaheim in southern California, settled down in a farmhouse, and tried to provide their own necessities. Pani Helena cooked and washed dishes, while the men worked the land. Occasionally they all went off on excursions.

One day we made a new excursion to the Santiago Cañon in the Santa Ana Mountains, . . . [and] stopped at a charming spot, called the "Picnic Grounds" (at present the Orange County Park). With its magnificent old live oaks overhung with wild grapevines, its green meadows and clear, limpid brook, the place was so beautiful that it excited our greatest admiration. Towards the evening we reached the upper part of the cañon, in the heart of the mountains. . . .

On an acre or so of level ground stood a tiny shanty, the dwelling-house; a few steps farther was an arbor covered with dead branches, vines, and climbing roses. Inside of the arbor a rustic sofa, table, and chairs, an outdoor dining room and living room in one. Next, a kitchen consisting of an iron stove under the shelter of widely-spread oak branches, with pantry shelves built in the cavity of the same tree. Some rose-bushes, a few flowers, a small palm, and an olive tree were the only improvement on nature.

This primitive miniature household was the centre of a crescent formed by a sloping mesa, thickly covered with bushes of wild lilac, wild honeysuckle, etc., and oaks. In front the grounds were closed by a swift creek, and a precipitous mountain, called the "Flores Peak." All around, like a living dark green frame, oaks and oaks, some of stupendous dimensions. In the distance, mossy rocks and mountains. The whole picture looked more like fantastic stage scenery than a real thing, and looking at it, my imagination carried me far, far beyond the hills, back to the footlights again.

A few years later we bought this place, and I called it "Arden," because, like the "Forest of Arden" in "As You Like It," everything that Shakespeare speaks of was on the spot,— oak trees, running brooks, palms, snakes, and even lions,—of course California lions,—really pumas.*

In 1893 I was invited by the Committee of the World's Fair Auxiliary Women's Congress, in Chicago, to take part in the theatrical section of the Congress and to say something about "Woman on the Stage." . . . Among others, there was expected a delegation of ladies from Russian Poland, but none of them came to Chicago. Apparently they were afraid of the possible conflict with their government, and they limited their activity to sending a few statistical notes—ah! most poor, bashful notes!

In the face of this obstacle, wishing by all means to have a representative of our nationality, Mrs. May Wright Sewall, the Chairman of the Executive Board, appealed to me, requesting most urgently that I appear as the proxy of the Polish delegates and speak on their behalf . . .

---

*The "colony" did not prosper, and Chlapowski, who financed it, began to run out of cash. Helena decided to return to the stage as her only way of earning money. She first had to learn English, but she did it in a few months, and afterward enjoyed some twenty years of great success on the American and European stage.

The auditorium was packed, and I had some difficulty in reaching the platform. The beginning of my speech was an excuse for the absence of my countrywomen from the Congress. I explained that they could not do anything so independent as speaking freely upon the situation of Polish women under the Russian and Prussian government, and then I sketched a few pictures of our existence, such as I knew and had read about.

Warmed up by the subject, and trying to arouse the sympathy of the brilliant audience for our cause, I was probably not careful enough in the choice of my expressions, but I said such words as my heart prompted me at the moment.

The people were moved by my words, and expressed in an emphatic way their approval of my feelings. Next day most of the Chicago papers, in big editorials, alluded to my address in a most flattering way, and added their own scathing comments upon the governments which had dismembered Poland, and especially upon Russia. Unfortunately for me, excerpts of the Chicago press were sent over to Europe and repeated both in the English, German, and Russian papers.

The result was that the stage in Modjeska's native country was closed to her and she was ordered never again to enter any part of the Russian territory. Fortunately, Count Bozenta and Modjeska had become naturalized citizens of the United States. They built a home at Arden, in Santiago Canyon. They spent their last years happily in that home and another in Newport, California. Rudolph became one of America's leading bridge engineers. Sienkiewicz remained in America until 1878, writing for Polish newspapers. His letters, in English translation, were published in 1954 as Portrait of America. *In 1905 he won the Nobel Prize with his novel,* Quo Vadis.

Helena Modjeska, Memories and Impressions: An Autobiography. *New York: Macmillan, 1910. Pages 242–46, 293–94, 512–13.*

20

Constance Gordon Cumming, Charmed by Yosemite

Constance Frederica Gordon Cumming (1837–1924), the daughter of a wealthy and aristocratic Scottish family, traveled alone for many years. She came to America in 1878 almost by accident. At Tahiti it seemed impossible to get a direct ship to the Hawaiian Islands without a long wait, so she took a ship bound to San Francisco, whence she knew there were frequent departures to the islands. She hoped to have a few days to look about California.

YOSEMITE VALLEY, APRIL 30, 1878

Just imagine those people in San Francisco telling us that we could see the Valley (*do* the Valley is the correct expression) in two days, but that three would be ample! Three days of jolting over the roughest roads—three days of hard work rushing from point to point in this wonderland, and then the weary journey to be done over again, shaking all impressions of calm beauty from our exhausted minds!

Well, I for one have wandered far enough over the wide world to know a unique glory when I am blessed by the sight of one, and the first glimpse of this extraordinary combination of granite crags and stupendous waterfalls showed me plainly enough that it would take me weeks to make acquaintance with them, and that if I fail to do so, I shall regret it all my life.

We had a drive of about twenty-seven miles from Clarke's

Ranch [i.e. Wawona] to this place, so we were obliged once more to pack ourselves into the vile van which does duty as a coach. They tell us that later in the season, when the roads have been repaired, they will put on good coaches. I heartily wish they had done so before we came: or still better, that we had arranged to ride to the valley, and send only our unfeeling luggage by coach.

Formerly every one had to ride, and the old bridle-track was led in zigzags along the face of steep hills, by the deep gorge through which the river Merced has cut for itself a way of escape from the valley, between rock-walls which rise precipitously for several hundred feet above its tumultuous waters. For ten miles the said track had to pass through a deep canyon where there was no room at all for a trail, so it was actually blasted from the solid rock, and at some points was led at a height of several hundred feet above the roaring stream, with no protecting parapet of any sort, but a sheer perpendicular fall, where one false step would assuredly prove the last. Along this dangerous trail, wise sure-footed horses crept warily, as if knowing that they were responsible for the safety of their riders as well as for their own.

Now safer though less picturesque roads have been engineered, by which the valley can be approached from several different points. That by which we entered is, I think, known as "Inspiration Point." When we started from Clarke's Ranch, we were then at about the same level as we are at this moment—namely, 4000 feet above the sea. The road gradually wound upwards through beautiful forest and by upland valleys, where the snow still lay pure and white; and here and there, where it had melted and exposed patches of dry earth, the red flame-like blossoms of the snow-plant gleamed vividly.

It was slow work toiling up those steep ascents, and it must have taken us much longer than our landlord had expected, for he had despatched us without a morsel of luncheon; and ere we reached the half-way house, where we were to change horses, we were all ravenous. A dozen hungry people, with appetites sharpened by the keen, exhilarating mountain air! No provisions of any sort were to be had; but the compassionate horse-keeper, hearing our pitiful complaints, produced a loaf and a pot of blackberry jelly, and we all sat on a bank and ate our "piece" (as the bairns in Scotland would say) with infinite relish, and drank from a clear stream close by. So were we satisfied with bread here in the wilderness. I confess to many qualms as to how that good fellow fared himself, as loaves cannot grow abundantly in those parts.

Once more we started on our toilsome way across mountain meadows and forest ridges, till at last we had gained a height of about 7000 feet above the sea. Then suddenly we caught our first sight of the valley lying about 3000 feet below us, an abrupt chasm in the great rolling expanse of billowy granite ridges—or I should rather describe it as a vast sunken pit, with perpendicular walls, and carpeted with a level meadow, through which flows a river gleaming like quicksilver.

Here and there a vertical cloud of spray on the face of the huge crags told where some snow-fed stream from the upper levels had found its way to the brink of the chasm—a perpendicular fall of from 2000 to 3000 feet.

The fall nearest to where we stood, yet at a distance of several miles, was pointed out as the Bridal Veil. It seemed a floating film of finest mist, on which played the loveliest rainbow lights. For the sun was already lowering behind us, and the afternoon shadows were stealing over the valley, though the light shone clear and bright on the cold white granite crags, and on the glittering snow-peaks of the high Sierras.

Each mighty precipice, and rock-needle, and strange granite dome was pointed out to us by name as we halted on the summit of the pass ere commencing the steep descent. The Bridal Veil falls over a granite crag near the entrance of the valley, which, on the opposite side, is guarded by a stupendous square-cut granite mass, projecting so far as seemingly to block the way. These form the gateway of this wonderful granite prison. Perhaps the great massive cliff rather suggests the idea of a huge keep wherein the genie of the valley braved the siege of the Ice-giants.

The Indians revere it as the great chief of the valley, but white men only know it as El Capitan. If it must have a new title, I think it should at least rank as a field-marshal in the rock-world, for assuredly no other crag exists that can compare with it. . . .

Each step in this strange valley affords a study for weeks, whether to an artist, a geologist, or any other lover of beautiful and wonderful scenes; and more than ever, I congratulate myself on having arrived here while all the oaks, alders, willows, and other deciduous trees, are bare and leafless, so that no curtain of dense foliage conceals the countless beauties of the valley. Already I have seen innumerable most beautiful views, scarcely veiled by the filmy network of fine twigs, but which evidently will be altogether concealed a month hence, when these have donned their summer dress. . . .

Here there is an enchanting reminder of home in the tall poplar-trees—the Balm of Gilead—which are just bursting into leaf, and fill the air with heavenly perfume. They grow in clumps all along the course of the Merced, the beautiful "river of Mercy," which flows through this green level valley so peacefully, as if it was thankful for this quiet interval in the course of its restless life.

There is no snow in the valley, but it still lies thickly on the hills all round. Very soon it will melt, and then the falls will all be in their glory, and the meadows will be flooded and the streams impassable. I am glad we have arrived in time to wander about dry-footed, and to learn the geography of the country in its normal state.

The valley is an almost dead level, about eight miles long, and varies in width from half a mile to two miles. It is like a beautiful park of greenest sward, through which winds the clear, calm river—a capital trout-stream, of about eighty feet in width. In every direction are scattered picturesque groups of magnificent trees, noble old oaks, and pines of 250 feet in height! The river is spanned by two wooden bridges; and three neat hotels are well placed about the middle of the valley, half a mile apart—happily not fine, incongruous buildings, but wooden bungalows, well suited to the requirements of such pilgrims as ourselves.

MAY 4

No wonder the Indians reverence the beautiful Yō-semité Falls. Even the white settlers in the valley cannot resist their influence, but speak of them with an admiration that amounts to love. Some of them have spent the winter here, and seem almost to have enjoyed it!

They say that if I could see the falls in their winter robes, all fringed with icicles, I should gain a glimpse of fairyland. At the base of the great fall the fairies build a real ice-palace, something more than a hundred feet high. It is formed by the ever falling, freezing spray; and the bright sun gleams on this glittering palace of crystal, and the falling water, striking upon it, shoots off in showers like myriad opals and diamonds.

MAY 7

Mr. John Muir describes several lovely valleys of the Yō-semité type farther to the south, in the heart of that "rugged wilderness of peaks and canyons, where the foaming tributaries of the San Joaquin and King's rivers take their rise." He found the most beautiful of them all near the source of the former—a canyon two miles long and half a mile broad, hemmed in by perpendicular granite crags, and the crystal river flowing through peaceful groves and meadows, haunted by deer and grouse and joyous singing-birds.

Thence he passed into a wilder, narrower gorge, with walls rising perpendicularly from 2000 to 4000 feet above the roaring river. "At the head of the valley the main canyon forks, *as is found to be the case in all Yō-semités.*"

Mr. Muir, however, attributes the formation of that valley to the action of two vast ice-rivers in the glacial period. But now the free, beautiful San Joaquin river, new-born from its glacial fountain, enters the valley in a glorious cascade, its glad waters overleaping granite crags 2000 feet in height.

Truly these Californian Alps hold treasures of delight for lovers of all beautiful nature who, on their parts, can bring strength and energy for mountaineering—a sure foot, a steady head, and any amount of endurance.

Fredrika Bremer (1801–1865), Swedish novelist and traveler, was in America from 1849 to 1851. She covered a great deal of ground and wrote, in some 500,000 words, her impressions of America. They were shortened a bit by her translator and published in two volumes as *The Homes of the New World* (1853). W. H. Furness, Jr., made this portrait during her stay in Boston. *(Courtesy American Swedish Historical Museum, Philadelphia, Pennsylvania.)*

Fredrika Bremer (1801–1865), a Swedish visitor, saw young women wearing the Bloomer costume in 1851 and thought it looked "extremely well on young ladies." It was named for Amelia Bloomer, who publicized it in her paper, *The Lily,* and wore it herself for years, as did many other activists in the movement for women's rights. This woodcut, by N. Orr, shows Mrs. Bloomer herself. It was published in *The Lily,* September 1851.

Isabella Lucy Bird, later Bishop (1831–1904), visited Hawaii in 1872, where she adopted a Hawaiian riding dress. She described it as "a thoroughly serviceable and feminine costume for mountaineering and other rough travelling," and she wore it through her adventures in the Rocky Mountains. Woodcut in Dorothy Middleton, *Victorian Lady Travellers*. *(London: Routledge & Kegan Paul, 1965)*.

Emily Faithfull (1835–1895), an English reformer interested in women's employment, noted that on her first visit to the United States in 1872 the typewriter was "in its tenderest infancy." The first practical commercial typewriter was invented in the United States by Christopher Sholes and was placed on the market by Remington in 1874, opening the way for the employment of many women. Sholes's daughter Lillian is shown at the keyboard in an engraving from the *Scientific American,* August 10, 1872.

Lucretia Coffin Mott (1793–1880), an American Quaker activist, was described by the Hungarian visitor, Theresa Pulszky, in 1851 as looking "like an antique cameo." The portrait was engraved by J. C. Buttre, for Elizabeth Cady Stanton, Susan B. Anthony, and Matilda Joslyn Gage, *The History of Woman Suffrage*, Vol. I. *(New York: Fowler and Wells, 1881).*

Marianne North (1830–1890), an indefatigable botanical explorer, visited America in 1871 in search of "tropical vegetation" to paint. Her photograph is as she saw herself, an unassuming English visitor. It was used as the frontispiece of her *Recollections of a Happy Life.* *(London and New York: Macmillan, 1892).*

Madame Helena Modjeska (1840–1909), Polish actress, in 1876 joined a group of compatriots to settle in California. Although she returned to Europe for a time, she and her husband eventually became American citizens and bought property in southern California. She was photographed in her garden there, and the picture was published as an art supplement to the *Los Angeles Times*, May 5, 1907. *(Courtesy California State Library).*

Constance Gordon Cumming (1837–1924) remarked in 1878 that the approach to Yosemite Valley by coach was difficult, but "formerly every one had to ride, and the old bridle-track was led in zigzags along the face of steep hills." The drawing of ladies in long dresses and wide-brimmed hats, riding the trail side-saddle, was published in *Hutchings' California Magazine*, Oct. 1859. *(Photograph courtesy California State Library).*

Constance Gordon Cumming (1837–1924), a Scottish traveler, spent much of her time in California's Yosemite Valley in 1878 sketching scenes, including this one of the Indian camp beside the Merced River. She used it, with other sketches, to illustrate her *Granite Crags. (Edinburgh & London: Blackwood, 1884).*

Constance Gordon Cumming, 1878

Constance was so entranced with Yosemite that she extended her stay there until almost the end of July. She rode and walked over much of the valley, sketching its views and becoming acquainted with some of its inhabitants. Before she left, she sounded a warning:

Indeed there is a corner of danger lest, in the praise-worthy determination to preserve the valley from all ruthless "improvers," and leave it wholly to nature, it may become an unmanageable wilderness. So long as the Indians had it to themselves, their frequent fires kept down the underwood, which is now growing up everywhere in such dense thickets, that soon all the finest views will be altogether hidden, and a regiment of woodcutters will be required to clear them. Already many beautiful views which enchanted me in the early spring are quite lost, since the scrub has come into leaf; and of course every year will increase this evil.

From California Miss Gordon Cumming took ship for Yokahama in August 1878. The following year, according to her Memories *(1903), she accepted the invitation of General and Mrs. Ulysses Grant to return to California. (An account of Grant's travels includes his visit to Yosemite, but does not mention Constance.) In a later visit to China she became interested in Hill Murray's mission to the blind; she is credited with inventing a numeral type for blind and illiterate Chinese. Her many books on the Hebrides, the Fiji Islands, Hawaii, Egypt, Japan, China, and India, all illustrated with her own sketches, made her one of the foremost women travel writers of her day.*

Constance Frederica Gordon Cumming, Granite Crags. *Edinburgh and London: Blackwood, 1884. Pages 91–95, 98–100, 109, 120–21, 241.*

21

Lady Duffus Hardy Satisfies Her Curiosity

Mary McDowell, Lady Duffus Hardy, came to America in 1880 with her daughter, Iza. Sir Thomas Duffus Hardy, husband and father, was, until his death in 1879, Deputy Keeper of Her Majesty's Records. Lady Hardy wrote novels, as did her daughter. The two Victorian ladies visited eastern Canada, New York, and cities across the United States. In Utah they wished to meet women of the Latter Day Saints (Mormons). The Mormons, who first settled near Salt Lake City in 1847, practiced plural marriage. The visitors wondered how a woman tolerated being one of several wives of one man.

SALT LAKE CITY, 1880

Knowing that the typical state of society here was utterly different to that in any other part of the world, we were in a vague state of expectation and excitement, and watched for some indication of it to come to the surface; we watched in vain. It was the same here as elsewhere. . . .

A woman is appreciated and respected according to the number of her children; those who have no family are merely tolerated or set aside as "no account." As a rule the childless wives live together under one roof, while those "more highly favoured of the Lord" have separate houses, and are more honourably regarded.

I visited one lady, the wife of a wealthy merchant, an English

144

gentleman who had outraged his family connections and nailed his colours to the Mormon mast, though he had at no time indulged in the luxury of more than two wives, and at present has only one.

Their residence is extremely beautiful; it is built in the fashion of an old-fashioned country house, with gabled roof and pointed windows, and stands in a large garden, beautifully laid out with rare shrubs and luxuriant flowers, a lovely home; the mistress thereof is a stately, noble-looking woman, with a grave earnest face, and eyes that seemed to be looking far away from this world into the next. There were two or three young children playing with their toys on the hearthrug; some others were having a game at hide and seek, "whooping" in the garden. It seemed to me that a whole school had been let loose to enjoy a holiday.

"Surely," I exclaimed, "these children cannot *all* be yours?"

"They are, and they are not," she answered, "I have fourteen children; some are still in the nursery, some are out in the world. Those," she added, indicating a pair of toddlers on the hearthrug, "belong to my sister wife, who died about a year ago; but they are the same as mine; they know no difference. Our children were all born under one roof, and we have mothered them in turn."

"This must be an unusual state of affairs," I ventured to remark, "even in Salt Lake. I should hardly have thought it possible that two ladies could have lived happily together under such circumstances."

"Nevertheless it is true," she answered.

"But do you mean to say," I urged, "that you *never* feel any petty jealousies?"

"I do not say that," she said somewhat sharply. "We are none of us perfect, and are all liable to the evil influence of earthly passions; but when we feel weak and failing we pray to God to help us, and He does."

"You are a strange people," I could not help observing. "In no other place in the world could such a state of things exist."

"Because nowhere else would you have the same faith to support you."

"But would you desire your daughters to enter into a polygamous marriage?" I persisted.

"If I could choose," she answered gravely, "they should each be the one wife to a good husband; but that must be as God pleases. Whatever their destiny may be their religion will help them to bear it."

Evidently desiring to end the conversation, she invited us into the garden, showed us her greenhouse, and gathered us some flowers, and we took our leave, having spent a delightful afternoon.

"I am afraid I have been more inquisitorial than good breeding sanctions," I said apologetically; "but how can I gain any information unless I ask for it?"

"I am very glad to have seen you," she replied, with a cordial hand-shake, "though as a rule I do not care to receive strangers—so many come with no introductions and intrude upon our privacy, and ask us questions, and then circulate false reports about us. They seem to regard us as zoological curiosities; quite forgetting that our homes are as sacred to us as theirs are to them. We used to be very hospitable," she added, "but now we receive no one unless they are introduced to us as you have been."

Lady Hardy and her daughter left Utah shortly thereafter and went on to their ultimate destination, California's Golden Gate. There they were impressed by the cable cars and morbidly fascinated by the fate of young girls in Chinatown.

SAN FRANCISCO

The streets of San Francisco are a wonder and a marvel. On every side there is an ever-changing, animated scene, . . . The attraction of the streets is entirely due to the polyglot gatherings of people from all lands, and the variegated tide is eternally flowing to and fro. Strange vehicles of all indescribable descriptions are dashing about the up-and-down stony streets at a breakneck pace. Clattering milk carts, travelling soda fountains, brewers' drays, sociable rockaways, and solitary "sulkies," their owners perched up between the spidery wheels, seemingly seated on nothing, are all rushing along pell-mell, helter-skelter. The streets are a perfect network of rails, and huge red cars, blue cars, and yellow cars, with their jingling bells, cross and recross at every turn. We look out for a collision, but none comes, and we elbow our way on.

We are jostled on one side by a Polish Israelite, in whom there "is no guile," with a long beard and high peaked hat. A moon-faced Mexican, with long hair, golden earrings, and red serape, walks in his shadow. A slipshod woman, in a grimy Oriental dress, flits past and disappears in a dark alley. A South Sea islander, a New Zealand chief, and a Mongolian merchant catch our eyes among the surging mass of European faces, and the blue-bloused, pig-tailed Chinaman, with his gliding, silent tread, swarms everywhere. He is always busy, always at work, carrying such weights as would set a donkey staggering. He has a long, hickory pole across one shoulder, and balancing at either end are huge round baskets filled with goods of all descriptions, enough to fill a waggon, but John carries the weight easily enough.

At the corner of California Street we come to a dead stop. There stands a kind of double vehicle, the foremost part being open, with a canopied top, seats running all round, and a man in the middle keeping solemn guard over a huge lever or crank. On the benches on either side were seated some half-dozen people, facing outwards, their feet dangling or resting on a narrow plank at their pleasure.

We take our places on the front seat, faces set forwards; a pretty balcony or wire lace-work ran in front of us breast high. The hind part was a common omnibus car, such as we are used to see all the world over. What magic would set the whole in motion? Of course we were going somewhere. There were no horses, no engine, no visible means of propelling us forward. A newly arrived Mongolian, seeing this strange vehicle for the first time, eyed it curiously, "No pushee, no pullee, no horsee, no steamie; Melican man heap smart."

At the sound of a bell the man turns the crank and off we go, flying in the face of the wind at the rate of ten miles an hour. We charge up one steep hill, then dash down, and up another, and so on for about four miles. Never was such a delicious breeze, such a flow of fresh, invigorating air. Long lines of elegant houses, some of distinguished architectural grandeur, with stately palms lifting their grand, green heads like sentinels on either side of the entrance doors, or rising from the smooth-shaven lawns embroidered with flowers of brilliant hues, fly past us on either side, their peaks and gables silhouetted against the bright blue skies. Streets and alleys, some wide, some narrow, diverge and radiate from either side of us. And through this vista of quaint habitations, of all sorts and sizes, we get such delicious bits of harbour and river scenery as would have delighted an artist's soul.

On we go, till we lose sight of sea and river, and the whole city unrolls itself beneath our feet, sliding down from its hundred hills, spreading in picturesque and panoramic beauty on all sides of us, till it is lost in the amethyst haze beyond. Whirled through the air by our invisible steeds, we look down upon church spires and steeples, massive towers and palace houses, on miles of streets, green squares, and blooming gardens, which Eve herself might have revelled in and dreamed of her paradise regained. With cheeks aglow, and spirits buoyant with the delight of our magic journey, we reached the foot of Lone Mountain.

Before we left our strange vehicle, called by the natives "the dummy," we ascertained something of its mysterious engineering. It is of similar construction to that in use for a time on the old Blackwall railway at home, being propelled by an underground cable, which runs along the centre of the road between the regular track rails, and the hidden underground force is controlled by the crank, deftly handled by the official who stands in the middle of our "dummy."

CHINATOWN

We pass on to the women's quarters. The Chinese rarely, very rarely bring their wives or families across the water; but they import large number of female slaves of the most degraded class, and for the most immoral purposes. These poor creatures have no sense of degradation, no knowledge of morality, but they fulfil the condition they are born to. . . .

We entered a long and narrow court with tall, dark houses on either side, so tall they seemed to shut out the skies; but in this confined space are domiciled twelve hundred of these female slaves, for slaves they are still, though sojourning in a free land, and by the law free agents, but the law is powerless to reach them. They are held in bondage by their own people and by the laws of their own nation. . . .

We picked our way through the dingy, deserted court, for though it was the women's quarter, there was not a woman to be seen. Some were evidently indulging in social festivities, for the sound of the gong, rasping fiddles, and screeching voices broke upon the silence of the night. Shadowy forms, like creatures from another world, stole by us with their noiseless tread and disappeared in the doorways on either side. We grope our way along by the light of our one solitary dip, and become suddenly aware of a dim light falling across our pathway.

We look round and observe an open grating about a foot square, and framed therein is the face of a Chinese belle. There she is precisely as we see her on our fans and tea-trays, her hair dressed in wings or fancy rolls and pinned with gilt pins, and profusely decorated with paper flowers of various colours, one half of her face being painted a bright vermilion in one blotch, beginning from the chin, covering the eyebrows, and reaching back to the ear.

On either side were the same gratings, with the same painted beauties behind them, looking out from the grated windows into the dark night. There sit those unhandsome, unwholesome sirens, like painted spiders, watching for their prey. Our escort struck a single thud upon the door of one of these houses, which acted like an "open sesame." Slowly and silently it swung back upon its hinges, and we stepped at once into a small, dimly-lighted room furnished with bare benches only.

Grouped round a tiny lamp upon the floor sat some half dozen women engaged in sewing and embroidery work. Other specimens of this unlovely womanhood in gorgeous celestial costumes were lounging in waiting attitude about the room.

The head of this establishment, a repulsive-looking old woman with blear almond eyes, jagged, projecting teeth, and a yellow skin dried and wrinkled like a piece of old parchment, welcomed us warmly in the usual pigeon English; the others nudged each other, and giggled and gabbed when we spoke to them, regarding us with curious eyes the while. Once, while we were taking a survey of things round us the door was opened noiselessly, as though on oiled hinges, and a Mongolian man's face appeared for a second in the aperture, but on catching sight of our party it disappeared, and the door swung silently to again.

There was one very young girl about fifteen among this degraded sisterhood; she was really pretty, a perfect type of Chinese beauty, with a delicate olive complexion, with a sweet, childlike, innocent expression of countenance—innocent because utterly ignorant and dead to any sense of shame or wrong, blind to the moral ugliness of the life of which she formed a part, because her baby eyes had seen nothing else, she had been reared in it and for it. Knowing no other aim or purpose in life, the mystery of modesty or purity was a thing unknown.

We shook hands with this child woman and spoke to her, but she only laughed and shook her head. We wondered how this young thing had fallen into this revolting company.

"Had she a mother?" we inquired.

"No," the ogress of the den answered, "she all mine, me buy her, her mother sell her for tlee hunnerd dollars. She velly good—she bling plenty money." . . .

We went our way through the silent moonlight with a strange, weird feeling falling over us, as though we had been wandering in dreamland, or living through the misty pages of the "Arabian Nights."

The Hardys made a second trip to America, described in Lady Hardy's Down South. *Iza wrote* Between Two Oceans *and* Oranges and Alligators.

Mary McDowell, Lady Duffus Hardy, Through Cities and Prairie Lands. Sketches of an American Tour. *New York: R. Worthington, 1881. Pages 115–18, 150–53, 192–96.*

22

Rose Pender on a Western Roundup

In 1883 Rose Pender (d. 1932) accompanied her husband, James, and Mr. E. Beaumont (presumably her husband's business partner) to America. James was director of the telegraph cable company which in the 1870s laid a submarine link from Aden to Natal. At that time Rose visited South Africa with him and wrote about the trip in No Telegraph; or, A Trip to Our Unconnected Colonies. *James's father, John Pender, was equally famous for his work in submarine cable and telegraph systems. The Penders, like many Britons, had invested in America's western lands, specifically in the Indian Territory Cattle Scheme. Their Neobrara Ranch, some 175 miles from Cheyenne, Wyoming, was on their itinerary, and they were eager to get a taste of the real Wild West.*

CHEYENNE, WYOMING, MAY 15, 1883

After nearly three months of continuous travelling, starting from New York, visiting Washington, St. Louis, on through dreary Arizona and fertile Texas, stopping at the quaint town of San Antonio long enough to see something of the country, then on to Los Angelos [sic], most prosperous of Californian fruit-growing districts, and so into the wonders of the Yosemite Valley; halting for a brief interval at San Francisco and Monterey, visiting lovely Lake Tahoe, with its snowy horizon of blue mountains and its fir-clothed hills, which the lumberers' axe

152

will, alas, soon destroy; introducing ourselves to the Mormons of Salt Lake City, and on through the wonderful scenery of Weber Canon and Valley; we at last reached our destination— Cheyenne City. . . .

An omnibus and pair met us from Dyer's Hotel, which considerate proceeding greatly surprised me, as I had been led to understand Cheyenne was still quite outside the pale of modern civilisation. However, I found this a decided mistake, as, indeed, I had found most of the information kindly bestowed upon us by people who knew no more of the West than we did. Dyer's was full, so we took up our abode at a big square building with good sleeping accommodation, a sitting room with a balcony and a piano, but with the worst served and cooked *table d'hôte* we had met with anywhere on our journey. . . .

The weather was, if anything, a trifle too hot; so much so, indeed, that I began to look rather with dismay upon my thick homespun Norfolk suit, and to contemplate getting a print dress, if such an article could be obtained. Cheyenne was a much larger place than I had imagined it would be, and not pretty by any means: no trees or shrubs, very wide streets, and some wonderfully good shops. I was able to get several useful articles of ready made clothing, including a chintz dressing gown, which replaced my felt one—which had been spoiled by the Chinese washing men—aprons, light shoes, a thick green veil, the great comfort of which I found shortly, and many other things I thought useful for our Prairie expedition.

One thing I could not get—a big white umbrella or sunshade; such an article had never been asked for before. Of course the shopman who supplied my wants put me through a thorough examination. "I was English?" "How long had I been in America?" "How did I like it?" "Guess it had surprised me some?" "What was I doing in Cheyenne?" "Guess English-women must be smart to undertake to drive across the prairies!" "Guess he would not do it!" &c.

As I found it far better to humour the curiosity of those I had dealings with, I answered all inquiries pleasantly, and having paid for my purchases, and exchanged a hand shake across the counter, I next went in search of the "lady" who would be so obliging as to make up a print frock for me. I had proposed asking her to wait upon me, but was assured she would certainly not do that. After a long search, I found her house—a three-roomed cottage not far from our hotel; and on knocking, was told to walk right in. It reminded me so much of the story of the Sewing Bee in the "Wide Wide World." Several women were seated all around the little room, working away and talking as if for their lives.*

My entrance caused no diversion, and I went up to one of the sewers and asked for Mrs. ———. "Guess I'm her," was the answer, with a strong nasal twang. While explaining my wants, one of the women got up and pushed a seat to me, for which courtesy I thanked her. Mrs. ——— was very civil, but in a manner which indicated perfect equality. She took an interest in my gown evidently, and suggested several modes, before I could persuade her that, as it was for very rough usage, the plainer and simple the style the better. After this was settled, of course I had to explain my appearance in Cheyenne, our past travels, and future route. They all seemed vastly interested, especially to hear I had actually seen the Mormons. I had to invent some pressing engagement to make my escape, and was begged to come again at an early date.

The party planned to attend a roundup on the Platte River, but as the season was too early they decided to visit Denver. Then they were persuaded to join an English couple in a climb up Pike's Peak.

MANITOU, COLORADO

Shortly after 5 o'clock we were up and preparing for the expedition. I wore a short striped skirt of chintz, and my Norfolk jacket over a flannel shirt. My boots, an old pair of

---

*The *Wide Wide World* was a sentimental and moralistic novel by an American, Susan B. Warner, published in 1851. It sold widely in America and abroad. The rural "bee" described in the book was a gathering of neighbors, not to sew but to prepare the harvested apples for drying and to make the winter's supply of sausages.

patent leather ones, worn for comfort in our long railway journeys, were extremely unfit for rough walking. In a very broad-brimmed hat and my thick veil, I fancy I looked the British tourist, as depicted by *Punch*, to the life. Mr. B[eaumont] would insist on wearing a Scotch cap, in spite of our remonstrances. As the glare of the sun on the snow would be great, and good head-covering indispensable, J[ames] took the precaution of carrying a large silk bandana; he had climbed Swiss mountains before, and knew what to expect. Oh, I must not forget my umbrella, a faithful companion, from which I never separated.

Our steeds and the guides awaited at the Piazza; I chose a nice little black mule in preference to the peculiar three-cornered ponies. It was a lovely road, or rather path, winding ever higher and higher through pine woods, here and there interspersed with an open common, covered with sweet-smelling flowering bushes. There were bears and leopards to be found, our guide told us, and in winter they became quite daring, and would prowl round the village at night in the hope of picking up a stray child—or something.

The higher we got the rougher grew the pathway. Big stones and rocks rolled from under the animals' feet; they slipped and plunged along, always excepting my little black mule. She seemed to have the feet of a cat. I gave her her own way entirely, and the art with which she climbed over or up the hillside to avoid obstacles was truly wonderful. A large tree had fallen quite across the path at an awkward place. The men got off and led the horses, but my mule considered a moment, then bucked her fore-legs over, and scrambling her hind-legs in some wonderful manner she got over quite safely and went placidly on.

By the time we reached snow-line most of the party, including our English acquaintances, had had enough of it. It certainly did look a formidable undertaking, and the guides were loud in their protests that we should not be able to get to the top, the snow was so deep. Some breakfast had been sent from the hotel, and this was then spread out. I declined to partake, feeling that I should require all my breath and agility if I was ever to reach the Observatory, but I wrapped up a biscuit and a piece of cheese and pocketed them, and secured a small flask of brandy.

Seeing we were determined, the guides then proceeded to fasten gunny-sacks to our feet. In reality they only tied them up in matting half-way to the knee, and they had not even brought matting enough, so sure were they that the snow-line would be the limit of the expedition. There were only five of us after all: J———, Mr. B———, myself, and two Americans, one from New York and the other, I think, a Brazilian. Our first climb was very severe and nearly stopped our breath; but after a bit we got better, and went along at a good pace, till we reached the last crown of the Peak. The snow was very deep and not hard, and often I slipped through up to my waist, struggling out as best I could. The sun was scorching, and I felt grateful for my thick veil and the handkerchief round my neck. The umbrella had to be closed, as it was impossible to scramble along holding it up.

Mr. B——— kept well ahead, the rest of us together in straggling fashion. The guide was of no help to any one, and at last threw himself down and declared he was done. I must tell you that he had remained behind and eaten his luncheon, fully convinced that we should all come back; but finding we did not he had to hurry to overtake us. Fortunately we had the brandy; and a good dose of it had the desired effect, and enabled him to get along. Presently the Brazilian sat down and declared himself faint from hunger. He had eaten no second breakfast. Some brandy and my biscuit and piece of cheese restored him, and on we went.

When not more than a quarter of a mile from the longed-for top I began to feel "done." My breath came in sobs—my feet felt like iron, and a terrible pain at my chest warned me to persevere all I knew. The telegraph wires now showed us the route, the poles sunken half-way in the snow. I resolved to go from one to another without stopping. Alas! I had to stop twice and the Brazilian collared me, passed me, and, to my bitter mortification, reached the door of the Observatory quite ten yards ahead! It was no use, I could get on no faster. I fancy we appeared forlorn objects to the two clerks who, poor souls, lived up at the top. It is the highest Observatory in the world, and the forecasts of the weather are taken from the top of Pike's Peak, one of the highest mountains in North America, 14,420 feet above the sea.

As to the view, I cannot describe it; it was wonderful! They said we could see for 150 miles over the Rockies—quite into Arizona, and I can believe that this was so. One peculiarity of it all was the striking clearness of everything. We could see Denver City, and even beyond, whilst Manitou, the Garden of the Gods, and all the weird scenery looked as plain as if we were there. The colouring was splendid. No words of mine can give the least idea of the glory of it all.

Our hosts hurried to make us some hot coffee, and to prepare us a meal; but we could not eat. The air affected us all more or less. I felt faint and painfully overcome with a desire to sleep, and we all had severe headaches. The only lively creature was a dear colley puppy. He did not seem to be at all affected by the air, and romped about in great delight at seeing new faces. The clerks told us they suffered terribly from headache, and were changed every three months, as their health could not stand the climate for a longer time. One of them died not long before. It must be a dreadful life.

Having rested for about half an hour, and written our names in the book, we prepared to descend. My gunny-bags were worn quite through, so I had no protection for my feet. Before starting they took us to an everlasting snow summit. When we looked down—standing on 100 ft. of frozen snow—into an endless crater, it made me shudder. One slip, and all would have been over! The remembrance of it comes back to me as a something never to be forgotten.

Of course, it was easier going down, but very tiring, and we tumbled into deep snowdrifts and struggled out as best we could. I was all the time nearly blind with a terrible headache. Glad, indeed, we were to reach the top of the last steep descent, and to see the timber line below us. I took hold of the telegraph wire—the posts stood about a yard and a-half above the snow— and, holding by it, fairly flew down, tumbling into a deep drift as I released my hold. The men sat down and slid to the bottom.

I was helped on to my good little black mule, which with the horses had been left tied up to trees, and we began our descent. I really cannot remember how we got on. I let the mule take her own way, and sat feeling bewildered and dazed till we got quite out of the pine trees on to the flat. The air by this time was no longer rarefied, and I gradually recovered. It was as if a heavy weight had been lifted from my head. Mr. B—— would not ride down. He tramped on and actually got in before us.

Great was the excitement at the little hotel to know how we had got on, and great was the surprise expressed when, after a good hot bath and fresh apparel, I took my place at the *table d'hôte* as fresh as if I had done nothing out of the way. . . . I enjoyed the whole thing thoroughly, and like to shut my eyes now to recall the grand view and the marvellous colouring.

AT THE PLATTE RIVER

We at last came upon the "Round-up," and a curious sight it was. Almost as far as eye could see were vast herds of cattle streaming slowly along. Mr. R—— calculated there were some twenty thousand. The incessant bellowing sounded formidable, and the appearance of the cattle was not reassuring, for though not large their huge wide-spread horns and wild eyes made me rather glad to be in the buggy. Really they were much too frightened to be savage, though at times a cow with a calf by her side, or when separated from it, would charge anything. A dog would be destroyed at once, and though on horseback you may ride quite close up to a herd, a man on foot would cause such a panic that a general stampede would be the result. We drew up to watch them cutting out some cattle from the large herd. It certainly was very cleverly done. Two men rode right in amongst them till they got close to the particular beast they wanted; they then quietly forced him along till quite outside the rest, when they yelled and shouted like demons. The poor steer, terrified, tore off at a gallop, pursued by the men. His object was to get back to his comrades and theirs to prevent him. Once they had got him up to the small bunch of cattle that he belonged to, all was well, but frequently he dodged them, and in spite of their frantic galloping, their awful oaths and yells, he got back to the large herd, and all had to be done over again.

I could not help thinking that were the whole thing done more quietly and gently much time might be saved, as the cowboys so terrify the wretched beasts that they become like mad things. However, the cowboy is a strange creature, quite unlike any other of his fellow men, and all he does must be done with swagger and noise. Their riding did not impress me. To begin with, the ponies are poor little things, about 14 hands, generally speaking utterly broken-spirited; and their saddles struck me as next to impossible to fall out of. Such a high croup behind, and a huge pommel in front, where the lasso is twisted—quite different from our saddles, where men must ride by balance. However, though I never saw any clever horsemanship, I was told wonderful stories of bucking horses.

I did not like the cowboys; they impressed me as brutal and cowardly, besides being utterly devoid of manners or good feeling. This was pretty well exemplified on our reaching our own outfit, where we were to spend the night. We drove up to unhitch, but though Mr. R——— was well known to all the boys and the foreman, not a soul came forward to offer to help us; they stood looking on whilst we took out the teams, unharnessed and tethered them, driving in pegs for the purpose. They watched me with a bucket and rope make some ineffectual efforts to draw water. . . . I mention this because we hear so much of the chivalrous cowboy and his great admiration and attention to everything in the shape of a woman, or "lady," I ought to say.

I *was* tired; we had jolted over a hundred miles in our two days' drive, and the heat and sleepless night and indifferent food were very trying. Still, I was quite prepared to enjoy the evening, only it was not enjoyable. Shortly after we had got all fixed for the night we were called to supper at the waggon. A fire was lighted in a hole, and some strips of awfully tough beef were cooked over it.

The cook was a poor bread maker, and the loaf more resembled dough than bread. A curious mixture of apples, currants, and treacle formed our feast. I dared not produce my knife and fork case, for fear of giving offence, and as the knives were cleaned by the simple process of sticking them in the ground I confess I did not greatly care to use them.

The coffee was hot and strong, and this made up for a good deal. I do not pretend to say it was clear, neither had we any milk. However, supper was got through, and then we sat on logs by the fire, and tried to get the men to talk; but not a word would they say, except "Yes" and "No." Mr. R———— said had I not been there they would have talked, but they feared their language might shock me! It was certainly a lovely and pictur-esque sight—the river glistening in the bright moonlight, the white tents and waggons, the camp fires burning at intervals for over a mile, the background of hills looking snow-white under the moonshine, and the huge herds of cattle, with mounted guard of cowboys in their picturesque dress, to say nothing of the herds of horses enclosed and feeding round, made up a scene I shall never forget, and which quite atoned for the discomforts and fatigues we had undergone.

After the roundup, the party traveled north to Deadwood, Fort Robinson, Slate Springs, Sturgeon City, Spearfish, Sundance, and Miles City, where there was a railroad station. Throughout her travels Rose never hesitated to give a blunt picture of the dirt, bugs, poor food, and bad service. But she was a good "Rustler," as the cowboys said. And she had a whale of a time.

Never in my life had I enjoyed anything half so much as our wild rough life of the past few weeks. The delicious pure air, the scenery, the strange sights and experiences, the sense of utter freedom and independence, and, above all, the immunity from any ailment whatever—a feeling of such well-being that to rise in the morning was a delight and to live and breathe a positive luxury—made our few weeks' drive over the prairies a happy time for me to look back upon for all my life. I may be singular in this—it is more than possible I am, and that to most others the roughness, discomforts and the fatigue of such a journey would be an insuperable bar to any enjoyment in such an expedition—but I can only relate from my own experience, and they were such as I describe.

The Penders left America after four months. James returned in 1885 and took part in a roundup whose crew included young Theodore Roosevelt. The severe winter of 1886–1887 caused heavy losses to western ranchers. Rose thought they lost at least half of their cattle. John Pender was knighted in 1888 and James, who was a Conservative member of Parliament, became a Baronet in 1897, making Rose a "Lady" until her death in 1932.

Rose Pender, A Lady's Experiences in the Wild West in 1883. *London: G. Tucker, 1888; reprinted, Lincoln: University of Nebraska Press, 1985. Pages 50–52, 56–61, 77–80, 123.*

23

Emily Pfeiffer in Niagara and Wisconsin

Emily Jane Davis Pfeiffer (1827–1890), born in Wales, was a popular writer whose poetic works were often compared to those of Elizabeth Barret Browning. In 1853 she married J. E. Pfeiffer, a German merchant established in London. They undertook a long journey which began in Greece and ended in 1884 in the United States. They planned to visit Mr. Pfeiffer's brother John, one of a group of Germans from Holstein who left their homeland in 1848–49 on account of political discontent and settled New Holstein, Wisconsin. The Pfeiffers also intended to cross the whole country and see its cities and places of interest.

1884

Our American cousins and all that pertains to them have long been so deeply interesting, so speculated upon, and so bewritten, that of them or their dwelling-place it would seem impossible at this time of day to say anything that is not trite. Once for all, then, be it understood that in the notes I shall take in passing I am innocent of all hope of adding to the stock of human knowledge. An American writer, Miss [Helen Hunt] Jackson, author of "Ramona," has likened herself, while conducting observations under similar circumstances, to a street Arab watching a procession from a lamppost. Almost as little science as such a vagrant might be supposed to possess, can I lay claim to with regard to much that will pass before my eyes; but in both cases it is possible that conscious ignorance may stimulate curiosity, and that the little incidents of the scene which are probably all that could now be new to any one, may reveal themselves more clearly to one so little encumbered with useful knowledge.

NIAGARA FALLS

I awake at the call, the soft thunderous music of the Falls, and, half ashamed of what I am about, pass the time between waking and getting up in framing an answer in sonnet form. Neither of us certainly has shared the common feeling of disappointment at the first meeting with this wonder of nature, although merely as a wonder it is perhaps easy to imagine that it could be something more. Figures and bold description will prepare the mind for anything in the matter of height and size; but the great cataract, as seen on this September morning, is so crowned with beauty, that one falls wholly subdued before it.

The shock we feel when we see that this Hercules of falling waters has been set to work by an Omphale, and is patiently turning a paper mill before taking its awful plunge, is at first painful; but I at least am an epicure in enjoyment, and refuse to yield the delight that is left, in storming after that which has been taken away.

In all the pictorial representations I have seen of Niagara, the object aimed at has apparently been to justify the figures. The artists have been crushed beneath the weight of the hundred million tons of water said to pass over the rock in the course of an hour, and have given no notion of the grace and apparent ease with which this task for a Titan has been achieved.

All the surroundings, if we except the paper mill, the horrible little railways, and the "elevators" which take you up and put you down in places where you never need to be, are of the tenderest sylvan beauty. . . .

From the observatory overtopping the museum one looks down upon the mass of water, churned to a snow-white foam, seething and boiling in the turbulent unrest of ages, of what are called the Canadian Falls. No tree or shrub, no crag of dark rock, no hint of a definite unchanging line, or note of colour, occurs to break the uniform pallor, as the vast mass of the united lakes leaps from rapid to rapid to its last mad plunge over the horse-shoe shaped height, and a part of it ascending in a vapoury mist, hovers as a white cloud, a departing ghost, over the wan, fiercely struggling waters. . . .

The side view of the falls from Luna Island, so called from the effects of Luna rainbow got from it, surpasses all. The torrent here flings itself full-breasted over the precipice, and as we watch it, descends, a sea of diamonds, into the arms of a rainbow, not now a lunar, but a solar one, a triumphal arch of light and colour.

It was curious to feel one's self in safety so near this vast and deadly power; but about Niagara there is a syren beauty which charms away all sense of terror. . . . The elements of the scene were in themselves anything but peaceful, and yet a strange peace seemed to fall upon us as we looked. Was it that the final catastrophe was so near at hand? I could not but think that these rapids, so fresh to the sense, so musically fresh to the ear, carrying forward the thought to the final plunge, would offer a great temptation to one who was weary of life.

NEW HOLSTEIN, WISCONSIN

It had rained at Milwaukee; later on it began to pour. E———— was uneasy about me, hearing that the vehicle which his brother John would bring to the station for us was an open one. I was distressed for John, divining how much he would bewail his want of means to do better for us. The train stopped, and we got out at the little roadside station, all in the heartless deluge. The poor fellow was in waiting with his twelve-year-old daughter Marie, and his rough, double-bodied, country trap and pair of greys near by.

Worn and white and thin as he had grown, he was speechless, even trembling with emotion. He could but shake our hands in silence, and look the welcome which his tongue refused to utter. Swathed like mummies in our many wraps and water-proofs, we ascended the buggy with some difficulty, and drove off under our umbrellas in the steady downpour over the uneven road.

It was a strangely silent meeting; the mortal years since we had met, and the heavily charged sky, seemed to be weighing upon us. The mile that we had to drive appeared interminable; and shaken and excited as John was, and his eyes a little dim with tears, I am persuaded we incurred some danger that night on the dark and rough bit of road between the station and his house.

At his gate stood a muffled figure with a lantern, the figure proving to be that of the unknown wife and hostess, come with her welcome into the rain. . . . There was just an introduction and shaking of hands under the umbrellas, and we were off again, threading our way through the wet bushes of the garden, mounted on the little wooden path or stage which did duty for the gravel. . . .

But in America we seemed hardly to be; this village of New Holstein—and indeed the whole district on this side Milwaukee—appearing rather a bit of the Fatherland transferred from the Old World to the New.

A sharper contrast than that afforded by this part of Wisconsin to Chicago it would be difficult to bring together—the restless ambition, passionate striving, unbounded hope, and worldly wealth of the one; the limited aspiration, patient industry, and frugality of the other.

Our stay at New Holstein gave us an opportunity of seeing life from a point which to us was wholly new—life such as is led in a locality which a few years ago was the bush. This entire region was covered with unreclaimed forest when John P[feiffer] and some half-dozen others, young friends and neighbours in the Old World, came out, bought land of from a hundred to two hundred acres apiece, and began life—the hard life of settlers—in a new country. Nothing less than youth, with its strength and hope and youthful love of the new and strange, could have tided men over hardships such as these encountered in the early years.

Little by little the bush had to be cleared before the work of agriculture could begin. Help was not easy to obtain, and the wages of labour so high that they would have swallowed up the profits. There was nothing for it but a hand-to-hand fight with nature.

The men whose youth was spent in such rude labour bear the unmistakable signs of it in their now advanced age. All of those still living—men of from fifty-five to sixty—have pushed through in some way, none have attained wealth as the result of their life-long struggles. The wives—all German bred, mostly German born—have fared no better than their husbands, their labours, as is the case with working women, being even more incessant than those of the men; and in addition to household toils, they have, most of them, borne many children. It is no wonder if they are prematurely aged, and if grace and physical charm have vanished before their time. These excellent souls are fully conscious of the hardship of such perpetual service; but, for all this, it is a peaceful, virtuous, and, as the world goes, a contented community; and since there is little ambition, there is little of carking care.

For people with the instincts and needs, material and moral, of peasants, and nothing more, such a state of things might be found the perfection of attainable happiness; and, indeed, in the simplicity, friendliness, and homogeneousness of the little society, there is a distinct charm that must be felt by all true hearts.

In a thousand ways you are made aware that the atmosphere, albeit Republican, is other than that of America, that, in effect, it is essentially German. The children learn English at the school, where all, Protestants and Catholics, are educated together; but few of the older people speak it, and German is the language of the home. German also are the large families, for those of the Americans rarely exceed two or three; German is the good housewifery, and German is that contempt of the body, of its beauty, and, in a degree of its health—all of it save the palate, which has always struck me as sorting so oddly with German thrift. The fare in these homely households—and notably in that of which we found ourselves members—is dainty

166

and far more cunningly prepared than we had met with at any of the great hotels since the Windsor in New York; and this appetizing *cuisine*, with its artistic *hors d'oeuvres* in the shape of schneebälle, sandtorte, chocolate and countless other cakes, is all the production of the ever-kind and busy hostess, and is of her manifold labours the crown and pride; that, I imagine, which entitles her to chief distinction among her compeers. What with the unwonted assurance of cleanliness, and the wholesome flavour of these productions—the sweet rye bread, perfect butter, milk, and cream,—the warmth of kindness, the long nights, and almost too long days of rest, I feel myself better in health than I have been for long, and am beginning really to pick up flesh.

I have said that Republicanism is here fully at home. Never before have I seen anything so nearly approaching to the ideal of equality and fraternity. There exists but one class; the servants even, though not dining with us elders, take their meals with the children. The result, setting aside personal habits, for which there certainly exists no ideal standard, is so largely a gain, that it appears with the kindly German nature to have led rather to a general raising of the tone than to that universal levelling which is elsewhere apparent. One is never met on any side by a word or thought which can offend, while of the poorest, which are all that stand for the lowliest, the voices and manner are as gentle and self-possessed as they are kindly.

It is a relief to find that there are balls, and rather frequent balls for the young people, since for the seniors, life would certainly be more tolerable without its pleasures! A drive over rough roads to a distant farm, and a visit to its inmates of from three to four hours, broken by coffee and cakes or by supper, according as it is timed, must at best be a ponderous amusement. But when the male portion of the company sits and smokes, uttering its thoughts at intervals in the short sentences which seem proper everywhere to the bucolic mind, and when the females of their kind renew in suppressed tones, undeterred by the awkwardness of long pauses, subjects which it might be supposed had dropped to sleep, the effort to keep up an appearance of enjoyment can hardly be pronounced recreative. . . . It is probable that the presence of strangers may have banished subjects the most congenial and suggestive, thereby imparting an air of constraint beyond what is usual at these meetings; but in any case, many consecutive hours spent in presence by two family groups, without music, without cards, without any influx of new ideas, any keen or experimental interest in politics or the course of the world, could never be very diverting.

For reading, where the battle of life is so hard, there is of course little time, and less for women than for men. Nor, as far as I can gather, is the imagination of these estimable people, upright and self-sacrificing as they are, deeply touched on the spiritual side. They rarely visit the inside of a church, and the schools, open as has been said, to Catholics and Protestants alike, are bound to forbear all religious instruction, a deficiency which, in the majority of cases, seems not to be supplemented by the parents.

Without aspiration, without dream of God or heaven, what in seasons of loss and sorrow becomes of the sensitive German heart? . . .

The elder people here, those who, although his seniors, have come out to settle later than John, when they feel to be very cosy and comfortable, continually drop into low German. The delight depicted on these faces, so full of simple kindness, when E——— replies in the tongue of his childhood, which he remembers as if he had never spoken any other, is only comparable to that worn by grandparents when listening to the lispings of another generation. . . .

The end has come to our peaceful and pleasant time at New Holstein. The parting has been too sad to dwell upon, only we have persuaded ourselves, and I hope truly, that the visit must be renewed at some future date. . . . We are thankful for what has been, and the ocean will not seem so wide to us now that we have once found heart to cross it.

In 1888 Mrs. Pfeiffer issued Women and Work, *a collection of articles from periodicals such as* Cornhill Magazine. *Her interests were in the social position of women and in dress reform. In 1889 J. E. Pfeiffer died and Emily never recovered from the loss; she followed him in death a year later. She established an orphanage and left money to promote women's higher education. Much of the money went to erect a hall for women students at the University of South Wales.*

Emily [Jane (Davis)] Pfeiffer, Flying Leaves from East and West. *London: Field & Tuer; New York: Scribner & Welford, 1885. Pages 81–82, 95–99, 104–110, 114–15.*

24

Madame Blanc and New York Working Girls

Madame Marie Therese De Solmes Blanc (1840–1907), a French writer, came to the United States to attend the World's Columbian Exposition held in Chicago in 1893. She remained in the country for several months to inquire into the status of women. One chapter in the resulting volume is entitled "Homes and Clubs for Working-Women."

Miss [Grace] Dodge's family is made up of working-girls. Her Association has more than a thousand members, who are all gathered together at the annual meetings, to which some hundreds of others who are interested in the work are also invited.

Miss Dodge belongs to the city of New York, and holds a high rank on the board of Public Instruction, being a commissioner of education. She established her Association of Working-Girls' Societies in 1884, in a bare room on Tenth Avenue. At first she gathered around her, without requiring any fee, about a dozen girls who spent their days behind the counter in a shop, or in working for factories. At the end of a month there were sixty of them, and they agreed to pay twenty-five cents a week apiece. The same Society now has a large house for which it pays one hundred and twenty-five dollars a month, sub-letting part of it for eighty-five dollars, which reduces the Society's rent to forty dollars, amply covered by the fees for membership.

As in other organizations, of which I shall find occasion to speak, there are classes in cooking, embroidery, and sewing. There are also weekly practical talks, which have been one of Miss Dodge's great means of usefulness. The subjects are very characteristic of American ways; for instance: "Men friends;" "How to find a husband;" "How to make money and how to save it."

One delightful detail is the fact that a sort of confraternity to help those who are poorer than themselves, was founded by the members of the Association as soon as it became thriving.

I am told that the spirit of imitation rapidly does away in these clubs with that extreme coarseness but too frequent among American women of the laboring class, although they may have attended the public schools,—a fresh proof that instruction and education are very different things. It is much to be regretted that all New York shop-girls do not belong to these clubs. The mere word to "serve" no doubt to them implies some degree of shame. The more ordinary the shop, the more aggressive the sense of social equality seems to be among the employees.

Now the club has this advantage: it brings persons employed in first-class houses into contact with poor beginners. Workers in jute, silk, paper, carpet, and cigarette manufactories are associated with dressmakers and girls from the best shops; and thus the contagious effect of example is soon seen.

The object of the Association founded by Miss Dodge is to unite, protect, and strengthen the interests of the various societies of working-girls, modelled after the first one, by collecting them in a single union. Closely connected with this group is the house on the north shore of Long Island, known as Holiday House. A generous lady placed this large house, with the fields and woods surrounding it, at the service of working-women whose health made it necessary for them to take a rest. For three dollars a week a girl may enjoy all the benefits of Holiday House and all the delights of the country. The clubs pay the travelling expenses; they all have fresh-air funds, and also arrange for this with the Working-Girls' Vacation Society, made up of rich girls, who, while they traverse the world for their own pleasure, do not forget that other young girls, tied down to their work, have neither opportunity nor means for travelling. They therefore busy themselves in finding out country farms where their less fortunate friends may find good fare at a low price; they obtain railway tickets at reduced rates for those whose families live at a distance; and they get free excursion tickets for those who have but a very short leave of absence.

In Fifteenth Street, passers-by are attracted by an elegant brown-stone structure inscribed with the words, "Young Women's Christian Association." I went in one evening. From the vestibule I am shown into the very pretty chapel, then into the vast sitting-room, which, with its comfortable seats, its sofas and its carpets, has all the appearance of a family parlor. I go up another story in the elevator, where I find the library and reading-rooms, containing all the newspapers and magazines. Here the scholars from the School of Design close by come to look for models; pieces of music and scores are lent gratuitously. There is a class in stenography and typewriting; there are also lessons in book-keeping.

Adjoining the house, with a separate entrance, is the restaurant,—rooms well lighted and ventilated, where women employed all day in offices, schools, or studios find excellent meals at the lowest prices, served on small tables with the utmost neatness. Those whom I see look like ladies; yet there is a crowd, each having to wait her turn. I see one girl pay thirty cents for a dinner of five dishes, including coffee. . . .

Connected with the buildings of the Christian Association is the Exchange for Woman's Work, which is nothing but a shop founded on charitable principles, and which exists in more or less flourishing condition in all American cities. Women of various conditions bring their work, which is sold anonymously,—needlework of every sort, from the finest to the coarsest; knitting, painted screens, lamp-shades, worsted-work, made-up linen, fans, all kinds of fancy articles and art wares.

One of the best-stocked bazaars of this description which I saw was in Philadelphia; pastry, preserves, cakes, and candies formed a large part of the trade.

Orders are taken, whether for dinners, wedding outfits, wardrobes for babies, household linen, or mending; every one feels it her duty to buy as much as possible. The Society take ten per cent of the amount of the sale, and the rest is sent to the anonymous work-woman, who is told, if she is not extremely skilful, to perfect herself in the trade-school belonging to the establishment, for only the most finished products are displayed. Private subscriptions pay for the rent, the lighting and heating, and other expenses of the house.

If the club and boarding-house are useful to all busy people who have not yet made a fortune, how much more necessary must they be to the working-classes! One often hears in New York of forewomen who are paid fifty dollars a week; of dressmakers and milliners who easily earn from two dollars and a half to three dollars a day in great houses which rival those of Paris. This may be. All artists are well paid in America,—the artist in dresses and hats as well as the rest. But not every one is an artist; there is the army of artisans.

Do you know that a mere working-girl on the average receives but five dollars, or five dollars and a quarter, a week? Now the lowest rents are tremendous; on the other hand, the tenement-house in the crowded districts is a den of vice and disease which defies all description. Situated in the midst of gambling hells, drinking saloons, and low-class dance halls, it affords its occupants but wretched lodgings,—so wretched that they may be tempted to seek refuge in the worst places merely that they may be warm. Therefore we can but pity the little working-girl who has no family, or who has left her family from that desire for independence which may be called a national characteristic. Her fate would be even worse, if help did not come from above, wholly impersonal, and so disguised that it cannot be confounded with alms.

Perhaps this feeling of solidarity which exists between rich and poor is more natural here than elsewhere in a society where great fortunes are made in the twinkling of an eye, and where many very wealthy people still have fresh in their memory their own years of privation. It is certain that one generous soul has only to take the initiative for a stream of gifts to flow in.

Thanks to these gifts, a home suddenly rises in a respectable part of the town,—a large house amply warmed, with broad stairs leading to neat rooms, possibly to chambers with three or four beds in each, but neat and of generous size. Substantial meals are served at convenient hours. All this is at the disposal of working-girls; it costs them no more than the mean lodging. They have books besides; in case of sickness, they are taken care of. They are perfectly free: there is nothing to prevent them from receiving their friends, men and women, in a real parlor, where nothing is wanting, not even a piano; and where little parties are given regularly, the only rule being that they must be in by ten o'clock.

Who can wonder at the success of the homes for working-girls which are now so numerous in New York, although there are not enough yet? I visited several of them, with which I have but one fault to find,—that is, they give a poor girl habits which her future husband will find it very hard to keep up. The condition for admission to these homes is, in addition to blameless conduct, the fact of not earning more than a certain fixed sum. There are homes of all kinds, there is even one for ladies who earn their living by some form of literary labor.

The Ladies' Christian Union, the mother house, in a fine part of the town, holds eighty-five boarders, and it is always full; the price of board supplies the table and housekeeping expenses, the other expenses being paid by the originators of the scheme. One branch of this house is especially devoted to shop-girls. There are even homes for the very young girls who pay their way by domestic labor. They learn to use the sewing-machine; they are taught laundry work and mending. Girls out of work may wait for a place in temporary homes at a low price.

Primrose House is a home for convalescents, for lonely girls whose wages are too small to maintain them. If they earn a dollar a week, they are required to pay twenty-five cents; if they earn two dollars, fifty cents, and so on; when they get up to more than five dollars, they are requested to go to some other home. All clubs are also registry offices. . . .

But I am really afraid of giving the idea that a Utopian existence is insured to American working-girls by the advance of sociology; this would be the very reverse of the truth. They struggle hard for their maintenance, in spite of the help given them by the churches and by individuals. However, their situation is improving daily, for the very reasons which have reduced so many men to the sad position of malcontents and unemployed. When the increasing and perfected intervention of machines renders the expenditure of human strength superfluous, the workman leaves to the work-woman that part of the work which requires only attention and skill.

Of course, women are content with moderate wages. Women earn less than men in almost all branches, from teaching to manual labor; we protest against this injustice, but it has thus far been impossible to remedy it. Is it not something, after all, to have provided so many openings which only a few years ago did not exist? There are now three hundred and forty-three trades at which American women can work. . . .

The lot of the best of them is as much as possible improved by the solicitude of which they are the object. Women are not allowed to undertake work that is too heavy or tiresome. The European custom of permitting women to work in the fields like beasts of burden seems to Americans barbarous. The idea that women should be employed in mines is abhorrent. And yet the system of tobacco factories and cotton mills is hard enough in its way. Many little girls begin to work at twelve or thirteen; the usual age is fourteen. After the age of twenty-five, their number decreases: no doubt marriage is the cause of this. The name "working-girls" as applied to them is therefore correct; they are for the most part young girls.

Madame Blanc was in America again in 1897 when she visited Sarah Orne Jewett in Maine. Her accounts were published in Paris in Choses et Gens d'Amérique *(1898) and* Nouvelle-France et Nouvelle-Angleterre *(1899).*

Madame [Marie Therese De Solms] Blanc (Th. Bentzon), The Condition of Woman in the United States: A Traveller's Notes, *tr. Abby Langdon Alger. Boston: Roberts Brothers, 1895; reprinted, Arno Press, 1972. Pages 241–44, 245–46, 250–53, 255, 257.*

25

Lady Theodora Guest Crosses the United States in a Private Railroad Car

Lady Theodora Guest (d. 1924) was the daughter of the Duke of Sutherland and the granddaughter of Earl Grosvenor. She and her husband, Thomas M. Guest, and a friend, H. Neville, took a brief excursion to the United States in 1894 to bridge the gap between the hunting season and the onset of warm weather in England. An American friend, Frank Thomson, General Manager of the Pennsylvania Railway, arranged for their deluxe trip across the country by private railroad car.

In six weeks, they covered the country, traveling over ten thousand miles, their car being hitched onto a number of different railway lines. For most of the trip they lived comfortably in the train, with the exception of the rough land trip into the Yosemite Valley.

APRIL 26, 1894

We began our travels, and going by the ordinary train to Philadelphia we changed there into our private car, which is now to become our home. We parted with regret with our kind friends, who had come to see us off, and then explored our car, by name the "Davy Crockett." Davy, though unknown to me till now, was a hero of the Californian and Mexican War.

There is some variety in these private cars, but as this and our subsequent one, the "Wildwood," varied only in details, one description will serve for both. At the extreme end is a covered platform, which you step on to, as you get into the train; off it, is, so to speak, the front door, through which you enter a sitting-room, all windows, with a sofa, two luxurious armchairs, and a table; a large looking-glass, bookshelf, little hammocks for papers, maps, and so on, and lamps. Out of this goes a narrow passage having on the right our bedroom, and a bath-room adjoining; next a large dining-room, sixteen feet by ten, in which we had all our meals. It had a sofa at this end; a writing-desk and table at the farther end, formed a sort of partition beyond which were two sofas, which made into two beds at night. Next came the kitchen and servants' room, and another door, a way in and out of the car.

Curtains and partitions divided the dining-room at night into a bed at this end for my maid; the two further sofas accommodating H. N[eville] and our subsequent philosopher, friend, and animated guide-book, M. S., leaving room for a full-sized dinner-table in the middle, and one or two of our luggage boxes, and chairs, &c., around. The total length of the "Wildwood" was sixty-two feet.

For this tentative journey we had only our three selves, my maid, Lawrence, our invaluable waiter, and Bayard, the cook; also, for a certain distance, Mr. T's own black servant, who was to see that all was right with the car, and to ascertain, I really believe, how we enjoyed ourselves, and report on his return to Mr. T. Never was such kindness and protection as we were surrounded with! for all this car is to be entirely to ourselves, and is, consequently, Elysium.

APRIL 30

We started on our real travels, or excursion No. 2. Mr. G. drove us down to Haverford, and saw us off in our new car, the "Wildwood," which was attached to a 9.10 train. It is rather better than the "Davy Crockett," being a little larger, more convenient and steadier, an important point, as we shall sleep many nights in it. In it came two of Mr. T.'s people, his secretary

Mr. H., and Mr. B.; they went with us to the first station, to see that all was right, and introduced Mr. S., who, Mr. B. said, we should find a "lovely man," and indeed he proved so. He it was who was to be our guide, philosopher, and friend, and to organise everything for us; in short, to show us America.

COLORADO SPRINGS

We now began the most beautiful journey, one to be remembered every Sunday of one's life. First, it was lovely to watch a fresh range of mountains appearing gradually on our right in the distance; as the Cheyenne faded in the north, this range, behind Florence, became more and more distinct; first the snow-tips, then the purple mountains, in every shade and variety of lilac and mauve, then the foot-hills. There was rather a rich plain on the east of us, as far as Pueblo, with many ranches, and good pasture and streams.

This town itself, apart from the beauty of its situation, is not of much interest to travellers being the center of the great petroleum and mining region; it has also large smelting and Bessemer steel works. Leaving it, our route took us westward again to Cañon City, and two miles beyond it we all settled in chairs on the outside platform as the train rushed into the Royal Gorge in the Grand Cañon of the Arkansaw [sic].

No words can describe the grandeur of this pass. For about eight miles the Arkansaw River has cut for itself a passage through gigantic walls of granite, which tower up on either side some three thousand feet, in many places so absolutely perpendicular that they almost seem to hang over the line and the river, the latter disputing possession with the railway, which winds round headlands of dark red granite, the river foaming beside it in tawny waves, "Like the mane of a chestnut steed," and rushing madly over its rocky bed, whilst we seem entering a mere fissure in the crags.

Narrower and darker it grows, till there appears to be absolutely no space for the track, which, by a marvel of engineering skill, is now suspended on the side of the cliff by steel girders morticed into the solid rock, and so actually overhangs the torrent. At other places, where there was no room for both, the track robs the water, and is laid on the bed of the river, which is walled back to make way for the interloper.

Where occasionally the gigantic ravine widened out a little there grew, here and there, tall solitary pines, standing like sentinels by the side of the rushing river, whose noise over- whelmed that of the train and made itself heard in useless remonstrance. This continued till we again emerged into full sunshine on the other side of the pass; and it is difficult to believe that there is anything much finer in the world. The alternations, too, of glowing sunlight as it caught the fantastic points which crowned the crags, and the deep, dark shadows below, and the indescribable beauty of the rich reds and cool greys of the colouring, made scenes which enriched for ever one's collection of memory pictures.

YOSEMITE VALLEY

We left San José at five o'clock, and ran for eighteen miles through a land flowing with milk and honey, in the form of fruit-trees and vegetables. At six we reached Niles, where the scenery changed. We traversed a narrow gorge, and emerged on a rolling moor, on a rising grade, and twisted in and out, and round the giant mounds of dark-coloured mould, partly grass grown, till darkness and driving rain hid all from our view; and we reached Barenda at ten, and passed the night in the station.

MAY 15

We rose early, leaving Barenda at six, and passing over an undulating plain, we arrived at seven at Raymond, by which time we were finishing breakfast. As we did so, we watched with curiosity a large vehicle more like a great boat on wheels than anything else, with charabanc seats on it; to this were attached four horses, and it presently drove up to a sort of high wooden platform outside the railway station, from which it became possible for us, by the exercise of great skill and agility to reach the box seats, which have been reserved for us for weeks.

The driver was a roughly got-up young man, in a sombrero, and large brown gauntlet gloves; of a melancholy and taciturn manner. Next to him sat I, on a high seat, with my feet swinging in the air, till happily large bags of mails were thrust in, and served as a footstool; and M. next me. Behind us were the rest of our party. Our seat was not absolutely uncomfortable as soon as I was balanced by the mails; otherwise there was nothing between me and fate, in the shape of the wheelers' backs, and a very low pole swaying between them, on to which I quite expected to be precipitated at any moment; or by any jerk; and the number and violence of those jerks are not to be forgotten, even now.

However, as we swung up a desolate, sandy track—for it could hardly be called a road—we got accustomed to the motion, which really was a novel experience; and the birds, flowers, trees, and scenery were beyond anything interesting.

There were many Woodpeckers, gorgeous Orioles, brilliant screaming Blue-jays, and, as the sun gradually came out, and dispersed the mist and clouds which at first were threatening, the drive commenced deliciously, but it was certainly cold. There were some Dogwood trees in flower, and much Chaparral; and Manzonita, (the latter seems to me identical with our Arbutus, but grows all over the hills like brushwood;) Leatherwood trees, with substantial yellow flowers, like enormous Primroses, all over them, and Buckeyes.

We climbed slowly up the mountain, a ridge of the Sierra Nevadas, having left the rich corn lands of the valley; and, ascending the rocky hill sides, we reached Depelas, where we changed horses, and then went on amongst Buckeye trees which gradually changed to Pines; and so to Grub Gulch, a name worthy of Bret Harte's wildest stories; and with some miners loafing about, who looked as if they had come out of his pages. It is in itself a pretty place, in spite of its unromantic name, and is surrounded by a mining district, one of the gold-mines being worked by electricity.

Going on all the way at a slow trot, though more generally at a walk, the four horses pulled and tugged our so-called "stage" round dangerous turns, up steep pitches, and down sudden declivities, crossing noisy little streams by insecure looking bridges till, at about 1.30, we reached Ahwahnee (or "the little valley"), and we were not sorry to climb down from our dizzy height, having been jolted and tossed about on that box since eight o'clock. Some of the company got down and walked about, in the few minutes occupied by changing horses, but it would have been so almost impossible to get back, had I done so, that it was more prudent not to move at all.

At the regular stopping-places, they have a sort of high platform of wood, and the men, who drive splendidly, bring their teams up to it so neatly that the descent is quite easy; and we gladly got down here, to find a warm fire, in a sitting-room, and a capital luncheon ready. We were not allowed to dawdle over it though, for in less than an hour the stage was round again, and "All aboard" was the cry.

We began ascending as soon as we started, and our flowering trees were now all left behind, giving way to magnificent Cedars, Sugar Pines, and Yellow Pines, straight as a dart, some two or three hundred feet high, with trunks like tortoiseshell; Digger Pines with feathery soft blue foliage; and at first many Oaks, Live Oaks (Ilex), Black Oaks, with their early shoots of a most delicate pink, and White Oaks. Our track, no wider than was absolutely necessary, wound up the mountains on a sort of terraced road, with very sharp turns, returning on themselves, but higher each time, looking down on Ahwahnee on its rich green plateau, surrounded entirely by the Pine-clad hills.

We went chiefly at a walk, but the coach swung round these curves with a fine disregard of safety; once our hind wheels were just over the edge, and we were as nearly as possible over, making Mr. S.'s blood run cold, as he had once seen a horrible overturn on this road, though he did not tell us the details till after we were safe back in the "Wildwood." There was much snow in the blue distance before us, but we did not for some time appreciate the fact that we should have to cross it, and that the snow would be a great hindrance. It had fallen here all Monday while descending in rain at St. José.

We took from Ahwahnee a team of thickset strong white horses, one of which, soon after starting, performed a series of most absurd bucks, like a jocund cow. This was a heavy long, toilsome stage; we had done twenty miles before luncheon, and had now to complete the forty-four; but the first ten took two hours and three-quarters, for after winding nearly to the top of the first spur of the Sierras, we got into the snow, and the roads became so frightfully heavy it was all the horses could do (cow and all) to pull us up. They were staunch and game, luckily, but it was very slow work; the roads, usually light and dusty, were heavy and dull, and every step was an effort.

All the time we were working through forest, the magnificent Pines becoming grander and more stately as we got higher and higher; the birds and flowers rarer. Masses of granite broke through the ground, in majestic disorder, and on we went, always with a precipice below on one side, and the rocks rising abruptly above the road on the other; and with these awfully sharp turns to swing around, and rivers to cross by bridges, or fords; but the latter were always easy, the streams flowing shallow and wide over the road. At one point, when it was beginning to get dark, we suddenly saw, by the light of the moon, that a great round boulder had detached itself from the hill above, and planted itself in the road. Was there, or was there not, room for the coach between it and the precipitous edge? The driver thought there was, and went on; but he did not reckon on the near leader shying at it violently, nearly pushing the off one down the bank, and it took the full power of the break [sic], and all the steadiness of the wheelers, just to swing us past in safety.

The snow got more universal, and, from scattered streaks, became a white expanse, and it was with a sense of relief that we found ourselves at the summit, with four miles of descent only, to get into Wawonah; and this, with four fresh horses, did not take long. We had changed the greys at a quarter to five, and came to our sixth and last relay just before seven. We ought to have got in at five but from the dreadful condition of the roads, we were two hours and a half late, and it was 7.30 before we drew up at Wawonah (the "Big tree.") . . .

We swung down full trot by the light of a bright moon into the little valley in which is placed Wawonah—a tidy little White Inn, where we had very cold rooms, a rather small supper, and a grand fire, in a sort of hall, round which everybody crowded, drivers included; and perhaps they needed it most. M. was much struck by the fact that though there was a bar, there was no evidence of drink; no sale of "half-pints" going on, and no tall beer glasses about.

We were not sorry to go to bed, and I, at any rate, was very tired and jolted to bits.

About one o'clock we got our first glimpse of the far-famed Yo Semite Valley! A vision of silver grey rocks of immeasurable height, and a valley far, far below us. Down the face of a rock we wound, with jolts—turning four times, then coming into a long, straight incline, with more jolts—just before us, a magnificent fall over an edge of rock, the Bridal Veil falls, eight hundred and sixty feet high, breaking into three lovely rippling streams at its base; on we dashed through them, and straight on some six miles more through a dead flat, luxuriant green and golden valley; all trees, flowers, birds, and rippling water, and the soft music of cascades, everywhere; and no snow at all. Our last four miles of rapid descent had left it all behind, and we seemed to have come with one jump from winter into summer. . . .

It was enchantment; and the extraordinary effect of this rich dead flat valley, some eight miles long by one and a half wide, entirely hemmed in by the most precipitous rocks, from three to four thousand feet high, was beyond what I had ever imagined, much as I have read of it.

But no description can ever do justice to it, any more than copies and photographs can to the Madonna di San Sisto. Every minute was a picture and a joy, and when we drew up, at about 1.30, at the platform of Stoneman's Hotel, I was almost dazed with delight mentally, and stiff as a rock bodily.

Several times on their crossing of the country the travelers witnessed crowds of shabby, desperate men waiting at railroad stations for transportation to Washington, D.C. All had lost their jobs in the depression of 1893 and were on their way to the capital, led by Jacob Coxey and others, to seek government relief. The pampered, carefree party in the private car, aside from some fears of being approached by men of the "army," gave little thought to the plight of the unemployed. "Nowhere but in America," wrote Lady Theodora, "can one experience such luxury, and I quite sympathised when Lawrence said: 'The Americans just idolise this kind of travelling.' "

The enterprising and convoluted nature of American rail transportation is reflected in the various lines to which the Pullman car was attached: the Pennsylvania Railway; Missouri Pacific; Burlington; Denver and Rio Grande; Central Pacific; Southern Pacific; Northern Pacific; Lake Shore, Michigan and Southern; and the Canadian Trunk Line.

Lady Theodora Guest, A Round Trip in North America. *London: Edward Stanford, 1895. Pages 25–26, 41, 73–75, 119–129.*

26

Annie Swan Smith on
Women's Clubs

Annie Swan Smith (1860–1943) published an English women's jour-
nal, Woman at Home. *As the United States joined the Allies in World*
War I, she came to America under the auspices of the British govern-
ment "to help explain to the American people the urgent need for closer
food conservation on their part, in order that their allies might be
enabled to carry on the fight." She spent seven months in 1917–1918
traveling across the country, and while her busy schedule gave her little
time for much more than lecturing, she was a perceptive observer.

She was struck by the phenomenon of women's clubs—something
almost unique to the United States. A socializing feature in cities and
in rural towns, the clubs laid the foundation for women's involvement
in politics and government.

I never came to an end of questioning regarding the women's
clubs which play so large and important a part in the national
life of America. We have a few women's clubs in our large cities,
but none in the country. Club life, as understood by American
women, is therefore practically a sealed book to us.

The London women's clubs, as known to me, are, with one,
or perhaps two, notable exceptions, mere places of rendezvous,
in which the real essence of club life created by unity of
purpose and community of interest is conspicuous by its absence.

Probably the true explanation of the failure of women's clubs to take any very deep root in England is that we are not really clubable people. The air of remoteness and aloofness which enables us to maintain unbroken silence towards one another through an entire railway journey, would probably militate against the central ideal of club life, i.e., comradeship.

I was beyond measure interested in the women's clubs, and as I was invited to speak at a large number of them, had ample opportunity for making pretty extensive, and in some degree intimate, study of them.

I approached the subject, I admit, with some prejudice, always remembering, at odd and provoking times, an adjective which had fallen from the lips of a highly intelligent American man we happened to entertain once as a guest in England. In reply to some question I put to him regarding the women's clubs, he described them as "accursed." I regarded him with a startled air, easily diagnosing some strong personal reason for his antipathy, but I was far too shy to ask for enlightenment.

I could not make up my mind all the time I was in America whether the women's clubs were an asset to the national life.

I spoke in a large number of club-houses in town and country, and carry away from these particular gatherings a vivid impression of vast numbers of active, highly intelligent, and extraordinarily restless women who talked a great deal, often to considerable purpose.

After the lapse of some months, I find that the restlessness is the dominant impression left with me.

Perpetually I asked myself how it happened that so many women who, judged by the ordinary standards of life, could not possibly be seeking to kill time, nor yet have much to kill, could afford to spend so many hours of each day at their clubs. Unless life differs tremendously from life in any other country, I could not just see how they did spare these hours, without neglecting or at least shirking something else.

A house cannot be run successfully over the telephone nor yet by merely giving orders to this one or that. It has to be pervaded by the personality of its mistress like a subtle but most acceptable aroma. The difference between a house and a home lies just there. It is the amount of personal care a woman gives to the infinitesimal details which some call drudgery which makes the subtle difference.

Many years of faithful housekeeping, which I admit has frequently interfered with some of my cherished aims and ambitions, entitle me to ask how it is that my sisters in America have so much time to spare for their club life? Are they better organizers and conservers of time, more efficient in the house-wifely arts, or just merely compromisers?

I should like to have these questions answered in the good faith in which I ask them. They have interested and troubled me a good deal. . . .

Of course there are clubs and clubs, the same as there are people and people.

What happy memories I have of delightful intercourse under the roofs of the women's club-houses of America, where I was enfolded by the warm comradeship of innumerable dear women with whom I had much in common!

What impressed me most was that they regarded their club as a secondary home, which was entitled to claim their interest and their personal supervision or rather participation in its communal life. Is this one of the articles of constitution in the women's clubs of America?

Never in a single instance did I find it regarded, as with us, as a mere convenience, or a makeshift, used oftenest by those who for some reason or another find home life disappointing.

I found the club women of America keen, not only in war work, but regarding most of the national questions, more especially suffrage. They were very kind to me; even forgiving, or at least excusing the feebleness of interest in women's suffrage.

"What! A woman like you not to be on the right side? What a loss!" they would say.

But whether a loss to me or to the Cause they did not specify.

One of my most delightful experiences of club life met me in a little agricultural town on the far edge of New York State.

I had travelled all night from the West and arrived at a little railroad junction at the discouraging hour of 9 a.m. I was met there by a woman about my own age, in charge of her own motor car, in which she conveyed me by a series of rapid movements over the worst roads in the world to our destination, her own comfortable farmhouse, on the outskirts of the little town where I was to speak. . . .

I was interested to find in this house no help of any kind, but just a capable, energetic, altogether delightful housewife, for whom every-day domestic duties had no terror. She not only did all her own work, managing to present a cheerful, matter-of-fact front, but she had time and to spare for intellectual pursuits. The living-room had its full complement of up-to-date books and current magazines, and there was no hint of poverty of soul in the conversation that ensued. . . .

After about an hour's comradely talk my hostess jumped up and said:—

"I would like you to visit with me in the kitchen. I've got to get our dinner ready."

This was a great compliment of which I was both conscious and proud. We retired to the kitchen where, over the mysteries of chicken salad and casserole cooking, we achieved a quite new comradeship of a particularly intimate kind.

It was an entirely happy morning, and prepared us for a successful afternoon meeting perhaps better than anything else could have done.

At twelve the man of the house appeared. We ate our good dinner with much appetite, and after washing up, retired to the meeting. . . . I only found then that she was the president of the women's club and chairman of the meeting. . . .

I received there an object lesson of the value of the Woman's Club in a purely rural district; how much it does towards compensating the women for the loss of town privileges. It provides a centre for their activities and a pivot for their interests such as we do not possess, yet desperately need, in rural England.

Annie Swan (Mrs. Burnett) Smith, America at Home: Impressions of a Visit in War Time. *London: Oliphants [1919?]. Pages 84–98. Also published with the title,* As Others See Her. *Boston: Houghton Mifflin, 1919.*

27

Countess Madeleine de Bryas in World War I

The Countess Madeleine de Bryas and her sister, Jacqueline de Bryas, came to America in 1918 to raise funds for the American Committee for Devastated France. They were born, educated, and always lived in France, but their mother was an American, a descendant of two men who were not only Signers of the Declaration of Independence but also framers of the Constitution of the United States—George Clymer and George Read. The sisters were tall, blonde, and blue-eyed; and they spoke English like natives—characteristics that surprised their American hosts.

The Committee for Devastated France was formed by Anne Morgan, the daughter of the financier and philanthropoist, John Pierpont Morgan. She had been an advocate of trade unions, a founder of the Working Girls' Vacation Association, and active in other social efforts. During the war she was much involved in relief efforts in France. The de Bryas sisters volunteered their help in raising funds.

We craned our necks to get a glimpse of all that was to be seen from the windows of the motor-car. Fifth Avenue! And this time we did indeed realize what New York in wartime means. The Third Liberty Loan Drive had just begun, and huge bright red-bordered flags were hanging lengthwise across the avenue bearing the words, "Fight the Huns," "If you have not bought a bond, you are a slacker," "What are you going to do to help the boys," etc., printed in enormous letters. On the walls of the houses big posters were seen, bearing expressive and encouraging mottoes to help win the war, such as "Give till it hurts." Then other posters were placarded everywhere, representing in descriptive painting "Pershing's crusaders."*

The war was everywhere—on the walls, in the windows, where little flags appeared with the stars indicating the number of men in a household or a firm who are soldiers. Most cars had the American, French, and English flags floating from the motor and another flag hanging in the window behind. Decorated stands were erected in different sections of the avenue and I could see women addressing crowds of passers-by, and from their energetic gestures and the attentive look of their audience I fancied they must be "hitting straight from the shoulder." This was my first contact with the speaking craze of which I was destined to become a victim!

Fifth Avenue looked so bright under its gay-colored flags that the town seemed decked out as if for some great victory. All this was perfectly novel to us, and we simply stared with excitement. No women in France ever make speeches out-of-doors; few men, in fact, do so, unless they are congressmen, and then only at such ceremonies as the unveiling of a commemorative monument. . . .

I got the evening papers and what was not our surprise and amusement to see my photograph and an account of one of the interviews under this heading.

"Countess Here to Aid Destitute. Sorry She Missed Raid on Paris. Mon Dieu; life is of a sadness! Think of having to spend all one's life explaining how it happened that one left Paris just one hour before the great German gun began the long-distance bombardment! Think of having to smile all one's life and

---

*America raised over eighteen billion dollars to provide loans to the Allies for the purchase of food and supplies. The "Liberty Bonds" were government bonds sold to the general public. Celebrities, many of them women, were recruited to speak to crowds on the street, in the workplace, and in every kind of group, exhorting them to buy the bonds. General Pershing, commander of the American Expeditionary Services in France, was respected and loved; his name was sure to rouse patriotic feelings in Americans, who subscribed to the loans in record numbers.

describe an ocean voyage of the year 1918 without even a peek of a submarine!

"That is the plight of the fair Countess Madeleine de Byras, blonde and blue-eyed, who arrived here recently after having systematically missed all the big shows of 1918."

WASHINGTON

Monsieur [André] Tardieu said to me: "I fear that you have come to America at an unfavorable moment, for the Liberty Loan drive has been on now for a week. It will last a fortnight longer and the American Government would certainly look on you with an unfavorable eye were you to ask for funds during this campaign."

"Then what do you advise me to do?" I asked.

After a moment's reflection Monsieur Tardieu said, "To speak for the Liberty Loan."

We agreed, and the following morning the Marquis de X———, a friend from France who was then on the [French] High Commission, took us to the Treasury Department, where we met Mr. Horner, the Director of the Speakers' Bureau.

And so it was arranged that for the next fortnight I was to work for his organization, speaking in Boston, New York, Philadelphia, and the vicinities of these cities, for the Third Liberty Loan Drive. . . .

The wife of the director [of Forest Glen Seminary in Maryland] came to fetch us in a comfortable motor-car (the motorcars are "frightfully" comfortable in America!) and we drove through Rock Creek Park. Never before had we seen a more picturesque sight. Washingtonians have let this park grow wild, without grooming it as Americans are tempted to do with everything under the sky—nature or themselves, specially. The creek to which the park owes its name is a noisy rivulet which we crossed several times at different points. The car simply dashed into the water, making a "splashy-bubbly" noise most refreshing to the ear in hot weather.

NEW YORK

As the motor-car took us through the streets we were fairly dazzled by all the lights, the more so because we were no longer accustomed to such brilliant illuminations. For months—nay, years—as soon as the sun disappeared behind the horizon, Paris had been plunged into darkness. Not a single streak of light was to be seen through the windows; few street-lamps were lit, one or two in each street, and as soon as an air raid was announced these were extinguished. Here, in New York, every effort was made to remind one of the Third Liberty Loan. Huge luminous posters, scintillating with inscriptions, urged the passer-by to subscribe. The city was lit up as for a royal reception; it seemed to be offering a gorgeous fête to its inhabitants.

Four days spent in Massachusetts, going from one set of people to another, seeing both the poor and the rich, the working-classes as well as the intellectuals, showed me that there was still great need of Allied propaganda to counteract the influence exercised by the Germans. The United States is a difficult country to manage; many and various problems seem to arise at each step, and I marveled greatly at the power that commands it all. I was told that this war is making out of the inhabitants of the United States the American Nation; through it, unity is being created. It is bringing together under the same flag the various nationalities of which the country is composed, but which up to the present had lived independently in this hospitable land, which ever welcomes adventurous spirits.

Nothing was of greater interest to us than the way in which the Third Liberty Loan drive was conducted here. One thing worth mentioning was the organization known as the "Four-Minute Men." Its members worked with incessant activity and patriotism for their country. They had thirty-one thousand members.

In each town a committee was formed . . . composed of volunteer speakers who gave their services to the government for the duration of the war. They partly gave up their business and devoted their time and their energy to speaking wherever it was judged necessary to be in touch with the masses.

They were then speaking for the Liberty Loan and when that loan was fully subscribed they undertook another campaign on behalf of the Red Cross, after which it was to be for the War-Savings Stamps, and the War Chest. In America, public opinion is formed largely through speech-making and personal contact with the people. I have seen nowhere else such eager listeners, always anxious to hear and understand what those recognized as capable of giving out information have to tell them.

I don't know how this educational method would take in my own country, but it would be interesting to put it on trial, for it might give unexpectedly good results; although I wonder whether our laboring classes would wish to listen to any speaker other than an advanced socialist. The press is the principal educator of the masses in France.

In the United States during the war the Four-Minute Men were, I should say, almost the principal factors in the moulding of public opinion. Their speeches, although different in form, were founded on the same basis, the fundamental ideas coming from the one source, The Committee on Public Information at Washington.

The members . . . were liable to be sent anywhere, to any town where their services might be required. One saw them wherever one went while the loan drive was on—in hotels, theaters, shops, in the open air, at factories. They are requested to speak during four minutes only, as their name implies. But imagine how impossible for a patriotic human speaker facing an eager public and with no one to call, "time's up," limiting himself conscientiously to the two hundred and forty seconds!

CHESTER, PENNSYLVANIA

"You will give an open-air address to seven thousand workmen to-day at noon. Not only are these men making munitions, but the Chester plant has already sent over to France the biggest gun manufactured so far in America, and is ready to send a second one in a few days." . . .

"You will certainly receive a very warm reception from our men," said the director. "They are wonderfully patriotic in their feelings, and this, I believe, is largely due to the influence we have exercised over them by trying to teach them what the war really means to America. You will, I dare say, be astonished to hear that six months ago not one of these workers could sing the 'Star-Spangled Banner,' nor did they even know that America had a national anthem." . . .

The man with the megaphone announced the "Marseillaise" and it was my turn to speak. Never in my whole life had I experienced such profound emotion as at that moment. The seven thousand workmen went almost frantic in their cheering of my country; and stretching far away before me I could see eager and honest faces lit up by the greatest enthusiasm. . . . I spoke from heart to heart with these men, not eloquently, by any means, but very simply, telling them what was going on "over there," and urging them to work hard at the munitions that were to protect the lives of their own boys fighting in the trenches, and to help deliver the suffering ones in my country.

The Third Liberty Loan drive ended, and the United States was "over the top!" Several billion dollars had been subscribed, and of this sum I am proud and delighted to have been the means of obtaining from subscribers one million dollars. . . . All through the Union, every town had subscribed far beyond the quota assigned to it by the Treasury Department at Washington, and as soon as each city had reached the financial goal a liberty flag was hoisted.

The speaking schedule laid out for the Countess was very rigorous. By the time the sisters reached California they were tired out. Madeleine had given over two hundred talks in six months, traveling from town to town, while Jacqueline served as her secretary and tried to protect her sister from importunate visitors and reporters. They wanted, more than anything, a few days of complete rest. They were not given those days, but they did have an enjoyable visit to the Theosophical Society's school at Point Loma.

SAN DIEGO

We were now so exhausted that our nerves were giving out, and simply to think of home and of our dear friends over there was sufficient to make the tears rise to our eyes. Even the sight of happy and healthy children broke our hearts when we thought of the sad and aged faces of the little ones of our destroyed regions, who had suffered from hunger and gone through such hardships that, poor mites, they had forgotten how to smile and how to play. In itself that thought was sufficient to make us feel that we must keep on. . . .

Never have I seen a more glorious setting for a school than the plot of land selected at Point Loma by Mrs. [Katherine] Tingley, who is the president of the "Universal Brotherhood and Theosophical Society." It is situated on a peninsula eight miles long and from one to three miles wide. We were received in the Aryan Memorial Temple, a gorgeous building of a radiant pink hue, by two darling little tots of three and four years old, who came forward to greet us with bunches of flowers. Then we entered the temple and listened to a symposium enacted by the "youngest teachers in the world," clad in white garments and wearing wreaths of flowers on their head. It was most amusing to watch those twenty or thirty little philosophers, whose ages ranged from three to perhaps sixteen, gravely arguing about the immortality of the soul and the necessity of mastering the mind and gradually controlling the inferior nature through the power of the will.

The school is a colony of about five hundred members, who have gathered there from all parts of the world, and where art, science, languages, philosophy, law, and horticulture are taught. The architecture of the various buildings is extremely original and due to the talent of Mme. Tingley, who built them fifteen years ago in what was then a desert where only sagebrush grew. The principal buildings are surmounted by huge domes of green and pink glass, and clustering around these temples are voluminous masses of palm-trees giving to the whole surrounding an appearance of gorgeousness, wealth, and material prosperity.

One of the most beautiful sights in California is the Greek Temple of Point Loma, built of white marble, where the Raja Yoga students play dramas. I imagine nothing can be more picturesque than to watch the actors seated on the steps or erect against the Doric pillars, through which, a little farther away beyond the cliffs, gleams the radiant blue Pacific.

The California climate seems to develop in the souls of its people a strong tendency toward spirituality and the search for divine wisdom. Numerous are the followers of all these various spiritual movements, about which we were given many pamphlets by zealous persons who hoped to convert us into active members of their own particular philosophical sect.

Here my thoughts reverted to Voltaire's witty, though perhaps exaggerated, words, "When two people talk together without understanding each other, then they are speaking philosophy, but when the one who is speaking does not understand what he himself is saying, then is he talking metaphysics."

On the day the two Frenchwomen arrived back in France they were greeted by General Pershing with the news that in three days the armistice would be signed.

Comtesse Madeleine de Bryas and Jacqueline de Bryas, A Frenchwoman's Impressions of America. *New York: Century, 1920. Pages 26–28, 30, 44–45, 55, 66–68, 74–75, 84, 225–27.*

Bibliography

WORKS CITED

Bentzon, Th., pseud. See Blanc.

[Bird, Isabella]. *The Englishwoman in America*. London: Murray, 1856. Published anonymously.

Bird, Isabella L. *A Lady's Life in the Rocky Mountains*. Norman, Oklahoma: University of Oklahoma Press, 1960. First published in London: Murray, 1879.

Bishop, Isabella Lucy Bird. See Bird

Blanc, Madame [Marie Therese De Solms] (Th. Bentzon). *The Condition of Woman in the United States: A Traveller's Notes*, tr. Abby Langdon Alger. Boston: Roberts Brothers, 1895; reprinted, Arno Press, 1972.

Bremer, Fredrika. *The Homes of the New World: Impressions of America*, tr. Mary Howitt. New York: Harper, 1858.

Bryas, Madeleine, Comtesse de, and Jacqueline de Bryas. *A Frenchwoman's Impressions of America*. New York: Century, 1920.

Butler, Frances Kemble. See Kemble.

Cumming, Constance Frederica Gordon. *Granite Crags*. Edinburgh and London: Blackwood, 1884.

D'Arusmont, Frances. See Wright.

Faithfull, Emily. *Three Visits to America*. New York: Fowler and Wells, 1884.

Finch, Marianne. *An Englishwoman's Experience in America*. London: Richard Bentley, 1853; reprinted, Negro Universities Press, 1969.

Guest, Lady Theodora. *A Round Trip in North America*. London: Edward Stanford, 1895.

Hardy, Mary McDowell, Lady Duffus. *Through Cities and Prairie Lands. Sketches of an American Tour*. New York: R. Worthington, 1881.

Jameson, Anna. *Sketches in Canada and Rambles Among the Red Men*. London: Longman, 1852. This reprints part of her *Winter Studies and Summer Rambles in Canada*, 1838.

Kemble, Frances Anne (later Butler). *The Journal of Frances Anne Butler*. London: John Murray, 1835; reprinted, New York: Benjamin Blom, 1970.

Bibliography

Kemble, Frances Anne (later Butler). *Journal of a Residence on a Georgian Plantation in 1838–1839.* New York: Harper, 1863.

La Tour du Pin de Gouvernet, Henrietta-Lucy (Dillon), Marquise de. *Recollections of the Revolution and the Empire, from the French of the "Journal d'une Femme de Cinquante Ans" by la Marquise de la Tour du Pin,* ed. and tr. Walter Geer. New York: Brentano, 1920.

Longworth, Maria Theresa. *Teresina in America.* New York: Arno Press, 1974. This is a reprint of *Teresina in America, by Thérèse Yelverton (Viscountess Avonmore).* London: Richard Bentley, 1875.

Martineau, Harriet. *Society in America.* London: Saunders and Otley, 1837; reprinted, New York: AMS Press, 1966.

Martineau, Harriet. *Retrospect of Western Travel.* London: Saunders and Otley, and New York: Harper, 1838.

Modjeska, Helena. *Memories and Impressions: An Autobiography.* New York: Macmillan, 1910.

Murray, Amelia M. *Letters from the United States, Cuba and Canada.* New York: Putnam, 1856; reprinted, Negro Universities Press, 1969.

North, Marianne. *Recollections of a Happy Life: Being the Autobiography of Marianne North,* ed. Mrs. John Addington Symonds. London and New York: Macmillan, 1892. A shortened version of her recollections, with beautiful color reproductions of some of her paintings, was published as *A Vision of Eden* in 1980.

Pender, Rose. *A Lady's Experiences in the Wild West in 1883.* London: G. Tucker, 1888; reprinted, Lincoln: University of Nebraska Press, 1985.

Pfeiffer, Emily [Jane (Davis)]. *Flying Leaves from East and West.* London: Field & Tuer; New York: Scribner & Welford, 1885.

Pfeiffer, Ida Reyer. *A Lady's Second Journey Round the World.* New York: Harper, 1856. A part was also published as *A Lady's Visit to California.* Oakland, Calif.: Biobooks, 1950.

Pulszky, Francis and Theresa. *White Red Black. Sketches of Society in the United States During the Visit of Their Guest.* Trubner, 1853; reprinted, Negro Universities Press, 1968.

Riedesel, Frederica Charlotte Louise (von Massow), Baroness von. *Letters and Journals Relating to the War of the American Revolution and the Capture of the German Troops at Saratoga,* tr. William L. Stone. Albany: Joel Munsell, 1867; reprinted, New York Times & Arno Press, 1968. A revised translation by Marvin L. Brown, Jr., was published as *Baroness von Riedesel and the American Revolution: Journal and Correspondence of a Tour of Duty, 1776–1783.* Chapel Hill, N.C.: University of North Carolina Press, 1965.

Schaw, Janet. *Journal of a Lady of Quality: Being the Narrative of a Journey from Scotland to the West Indies, North Carolina and Portugal, in the Years 1774 to 1776,* ed. Evangeline Walker Andrews, in collaboration with Charles McLean Andrews. New Haven: Yale University Press, 1923.

Bibliography

Smith, Annie Swan (Mrs. Burnett). *America at Home: Impressions of a Visit in War Time*. London: Oliphants [1919?]. Also published with the title, *As Others See Her*. Boston: Houghton Mifflin, 1919.

Swan, Annie. See Smith.

Trollope, Frances. *Domestic Manners of the Americans*. New York: Whittaker, Treacher, & Co., 1832.

Wright, Frances (later D'Arusmont). *Views of Society and Manners in America*. London: Longman, Hurst, Rees, Orme and Brown, 1821.

Yelverton, Therese, Viscountess Avonmore. See Longworth.

WORKS CONTAINING ACCOUNTS BY EUROPEAN WOMEN VISITORS TO AMERICA

Adams, Percy G., ed. *Travel Literature through the Ages. An Anthology*. New York & London: Garland, 1988. Frances Trollope.

Baker, William J., ed. *America Perceived: A View from Abroad in the 19th Century*. West Haven, Conn.: Pendulum Press, 1974. Fredrika Bremer, Francis and Theresa Pulszky, Frances Trollope, Frances Kemble, Isabella Bird, and Emily Faithfull.

Bartel, Roland, and E. R. Bingham. *America through Foreign Eyes, 1827–1842: Selected Source Materials*. Boston: D. C. Heath, 1956. Frances Trollope.

Bennett, E. D., ed. *American Journeys: An Anthology of Travel in the United States*. Convent Station, N.J., 1975. Isabella Bird.

Commager, Henry Steele, ed. *America in Perspective: The United States through Foreign Eyes*. New York: Random House, 1947. Harriet Martineau and Francis and Theresa Pulszky.

Eaton, Clement, ed. *The Leaven of Democracy: The Growth of the Democratic Spirit in the Time of Jackson*. New York: Braziller, 1963. Margaret Hall, Harriet Martineau, Fredrika Bremer, and Frances Trollope.

Handlin, Oscar, ed. *This Was America, . . . As Recorded by European Travelers to the Western Shore in the 18th, 19th, and 20th Centuries*. Cambridge: Harvard University Press, 1949. Fredrika Bremer, Francis and Theresa Pulszky, Alma Isabel Sofia Hedin, and Odette Keun.

Nevin, Allan, comp. and ed. *American Social History as Recorded by British Travellers*. New York: Holt, 1923. Reissued as *America through British Eyes*, 1948. Frances Trollope, Harriet Martineau, and Fanny Kemble.

Newby, Eric, comp. *A Book of Travellers' Tales*. New York: Viking, 1985. Janet Schaw, Frances Trollope, Fanny Kemble, and Isabella Bird.

Index

Index

Galata, Sisters of Mercy at, 110
Garibaldi, 77
Gates, General Horatio, 10, 12, 13
Geneva, New York, 65
Georgia, xvi, 46, 48–55
Germany, 15
Grand Canyon of the Arkansas, 178–79
Grant, Ulysses, and family, 116–17, 143
Great Britain, philanthropists, 102
Grosvenor, Earl, 176
"Grundy, Mrs.," 132
Grub Gulch, 180
Guest, Lady Theodora, xiii–xiv, xv, 176–84
Guest, Thomas, 176
Gurney, Mr. and Mrs. Russell, 116, 117

Haiti, 31
Hardy, Iza, 144
Hardy, Lady Duffus, 144–51
Hardy, Sir Thomas Duffus, 144
Harte, Bret, 180
Hawaii, 97, 125, 128, 138
Health, 35, 50–53, 84, 128
Hervieu, Auguste, 32, 36
Hetch-Hetchy, 106, 142
Hicks, Elias, 73
Hicksite Quakers, 72–73
Hogg, Mr., 5
Holiday House, 171
Holstein, Germany, 162
Horner, Mr., 191
Horses, xv, 120, 129, 139, 155, 159, 180–83
Houghton, Mifflin & Co., 123
Housekeeping, 186–87
Hughes, Dr., and family, 131–32
Hungary, 70, 71: Revolution, xii
Hunt, Harriot, 68, 82
Husking bee, 22
Hutchings' Hotel, Yosemite, 110

Indian Territory Cattle Scheme, 152
Indian tribes: Chippewas, 56–58; Delaware, 60; Great Lakes, 56;

Mohawk, 17; Onondaga, 17; Otoe, 75; Rogue River, Oregon, 88–89
Indian women, status, 58–60
Indians, xiv, xv, 11, 17, 19, 32, 36–37, 93, 142–43: at White House, 75–76; California, 83–90; in the Northwest, 58–60; in Yosemite, 106; treatment of, 60–61. See also Indian tribes
Ireland, xiii

Jackson, Helen Hunt, 162
Jamaica, 117
Jameson, Anna, xiv, 56–62
Jameson, Robert, 56
Japan, 118
Jefferson, Thomas, 28, 74
Jewett, Sarah Orne, 175
Johnston, Charlotte (Neengai), 56–57
Johnston, George, 56
Johnston, John, 56
Judith, a slave, 23

Karwowski, Dr., 134
Kemble, Charles, 46
Kemble, Frances (Fanny), xii, xvi, 46–55
Kentucky, 95–96
King, Mr., overseer, 52
King's River, 142
Knitting, 129
Kossuth, Louis, xii, 70, 71, 72, 77

La Tour du Pin, Frédéric, Count de, 16–22
La Tour du Pin, Henrietta, Countess de, xiv, 16–25
La Tour du Pin, Humbert, 16
La Tour du Pin, Séraphine, 16, 21
Ladies' Christian Union, 173
Lake Tahoe, 152–53
Lake Huron, 62
Landscapes, xiii
Latter-Day Saints. See Mormons
Laundries, 123
Lawrence, Mary Viola, 110
Lecturing, 82, 185–88, 189–96
Lee, Ann, 19